Maestro

By the same author:

FOR THE LOVE OF GOLF: THE BEST OF DOBEREINER
THE SAME WITH THE HOLE IN IT
GOLF RULES EXPLAINED

Maestro

The Life of Sir Henry Cotton

PETER DOBEREINER

Hodder & Stoughton
LONDON SYDNEY AUCKLAND

British Library Cataloguing in Publication Data

Dobereiner, Peter
  Maestro: The life of Henry Cotton.
  I. Title
  796.352092

  ISBN 0-340-59418-7

First published in Great Britain in 1992 by Hodder and Stoughton Ltd
This edition 1993

Published by Hodder and Stoughton,
a division of Hodder and Stoughton Ltd,
Mill Road, Dunton Green, Sevenoaks, Kent TN13 2YA.
Editorial Office: 47 Bedford Square, London WC1B 3DP.

Designed by Behram Kapadia.

Photoset by E.P.L. BookSet, Norwood, London.

Printed in Great Britain by St Edmundsbury Press,
Bury St Edmunds, Suffolk.

Maestro

Contents

Introduction by Laddie Lucas

Sir Henry Cotton's life, which makes one of the most compelling human interest stories of modern times, is remarkable for three prime features.

First, it changed, in a decade, and often amid vehement controversy, the image and status of a long-established and, in a class sense, subservient profession. Second, it achieved by example, personal regimen and endeavour an all-round standard which its contemporary characters had either never contemplated or had regarded as being far out of reach. Third, its fame endured, in its successive and distinctive phases, for – literally – a lifetime.

The subject of this definitive biography was being talked, argued and written about long after his highly-publicised playing days were over. He was 'news' in his twenties and he remained 'news' in his seventies. Right up to the end of his life he cultivated and, usually by design, provoked 'talking points'. Seldom was he out of the public's gaze.

What a story it was and how effectively has the biographer now told it! Peter Dobereiner, with his arresting prose style, his eye for the unusual, his humour and his understanding of the human frame (particularly when it is contorted with a golf club in its hands), has provided just the narrative which Cotton's extraordinary career deserves. For an old friend of the Maestro, the result inevitably sets the mind racing back over the years to savour again the events which are still cut deeply – and gratefully – in the memory.

My first, fleeting contact with Cotton was at the Open championship at Muirfield in 1935. He was the defending champion

1

and I, an apprehensive freshman entrant from a university. On the practice days before the championship I used to find out from Cotton's caddie when his employer would be hitting balls on the practice ground. Then I would walk over, sit down on the grass and watch him 'go through the bag'. I could still describe the well-cut clothes he wore. Toots, his wife-soon-to-be, her short figure perched on a shooting stick, held a silent watch over each session.

The process seldom took more than twenty or twenty-five minutes. The player had done all his practising at home well before he arrived at Muirfield. As he walked away from the practice ground each time, I badly wanted to speak to him; but I could never find the courage to try it. His conversation with Toots, his caddie and the few interlopers who were always about, was loud, staccato and pretty tart. It did not encourage intervention. Anyway, heroes are best kept at arm's length.

Came the Friday and the last day of the championship when, in those days, the final 36 holes were played. As I walked off the 18th green after my third round, I looked up at the scoreboard. On 219, I was lying seventh overall, one shot behind Cotton and one in front of Lawson Little, the American and British amateur champion, with whom I was battling for the low amateur prize. In my youthful ignorance, I couldn't see any reason why I should not do 70 or 71 after lunch.

I took 81. As I walked away from the club by myself, grip in one hand and clubs slung over the shoulder, tears were very close. Just then, Cotton crossed my path on his way to his big red Mercedes. He was obviously displeased with his poor last round of 75. Toots was stumping along beside him.

He turned momentarily towards me as he passed. "Sorry to see you took a lot this afternoon. I know how you'll be feeling. But never mind, you will have learnt from it. Why not get in touch and we'll have some games together?"

He and Toots were gone before I could manage a rejoinder. I couldn't believe he knew who I was. But a ray of sunshine had pierced the overcast. It turned out to be the start of a friendship valued, I like to think, as much by the one as by the other.

The following summer, I went out to Brussels with two close friends to spend a fortnight with Cotton at Waterloo where he was then based. The programme was always the same each day. We all hit balls with him for two hours in the morning and then played 18 holes after lunch. Toots usually came in to make it a five-ball.

The members behind us never seemed to mind. They regarded Cotton as God. If we went out to a fashionable restaurant to dine in the evening, the people at the tables near by stood up as he entered. But mostly we dined at his home which Toots had furnished with exceptional taste and where she kept a table the like of which could not have been bettered in Brussels.

We played fourteen rounds at Waterloo, a course of some 6,700 yards, during our visit. We went off the furthest back tees and every putt was holed out. Henry never missed a fairway from the tee and he never took more than 67.

He had, by then, just made a huge change in his swing. It is worth describing it in detail for, as far as I know, he never wrote about it nor did he ever speak about it except to his few intimates who were also his disciples. He guarded it like the Ultra Secret. Most of the great players, past and present, have had to make big changes in their actions to get to the top *and stay there*. But, usually, they've been quite open about it. Not so Cotton.

When he won the championship at Sandwich in 1934 he was, he knew, vulnerable in a right-to-left wind. With his always weak left-hand grip, he had started his professional career as a fader of the ball. Then he went to the United States and, as his biographer makes clear, found that Tommy Armour and the rest of the leading tournament players there were drawing the ball from right to left and hitting it further.

He decided to do likewise, but soon after Sandwich – in 1935 and early 1936 – he concluded he would never achieve the absolute mastery he sought over the flight of a golf ball along that road. And the ability to flight the ball – to move it about at will – to suit all winds and conditions became, for him, the Eldorado for which he strove.

He had always taken the club back flat and well inside and his hands at the top of the backswing remained relatively flat, i.e. barely above the level of his shoulders with the club-face not as open as it subsequently became. Now he made, off his own bat and without any prompting from anyone, the massive change which took him to the summit.

He still took the club back well inside but as it moved up towards the top he began, he said, to get his hands deliberately up and into a more upright and open position with the left wrist more under the shaft and the club-face itself well open, i.e. with the toe pointing downwards. He confided that he had to be conscious at the top that his hands were "up and forward" with the shaft of the club "not so much across the top of the back as forward almost above the neck". That was, he said, the latent feeling he was always striving for – the feeling that was to lift his striking into the highest class.

From this upright and open position at the top, he contended he could hit the ball "as early as you like without any fear of hooking it". Hitting the ball early from an open and relatively upright position at the top – releasing the club, as he put it, early from the top – now became the aim to end all aims in his swing. But he remained ever secretive about his discovery. With it he became confident that he could flight the ball and move it about any way he wanted. It was noticeable to his disciples that he began to judge his contemporaries by their ability to flight the ball – "to throw the ball up, boy, with a long iron or a wooden club: a lot of them drive the ball low and can't do it".

From all this flowed his doctrine that to play good, consistent golf in the highest class "you must, boy, know the angles and the extremes of your swing and what they give you. Only then can you find a balance." Thereafter, he never deviated from these principles.

The only player Henry ever looked up to in the great days of the late 1930s was Harry Vardon, six times Open champion. "Old Harry," he used to say, was the purest striker of the lot "because he hit it earlier than the rest – hit the ball early *with the club-head*". That was also, he said, why Vardon took so little turf with his irons.

After this change, which took him (under Toots' ever vigilant eye) some eighteen months to perfect, there wasn't another contemporary striker, British or American, to touch him. He didn't win the 1936 championship at Hoylake (he was equal third), but his hitting in that Open was, he said, consistently the best he had yet achieved. A friend of mine, one of the game's best judges, saw much of it. "My dear," he exclaimed afterwards, "Henry's striking at Hoylake was so exquisite it was enough to induce a sexual orgasm!"

I doubt whether more than a handful will remember today just how good a golfer Cotton became in the last years of the 1930s as Europe slipped relentlessly into war. I saw every shot he hit in his last victorious round at Carnoustie in 1937 when, as Peter Dobereiner so well recalls, he beat off the weight of a very good

US Ryder Cup team with a brand of golf which set him apart. People wondered then why he didn't go to the States to pit his skills against the Americans. Some even suggested he funked it to avoid the risk of damaging his reputation. The answer, in fact, was purely financial. Give or take a dime, there were, at the ruling exchange rate of the day, five dollars to every pound sterling. Much better, then, to be paid in pounds than in dollars. Toots saw to that. "Let them come here," she cried, "if they want to take Henry."

Paradoxically, I never thought Cotton was a good teacher of the game. He taught it as he himself had learnt it, and that wasn't necessarily what others needed. But to play with, or up against him at his very best was an exhilarating experience. His rhythm was infectious, his extrovert enthusiasm for the game, and for perfection, contagious. I remember John Jacobs once telling me how, as a boy of thirteen, he had seen Henry play much of his fine two final rounds in the Open at St George's in 1938, the year of the Great Gale.

"Henry didn't win," he said, "but for umpteen years after that every time I played golf I was Henry Cotton." That was the captivating influence of the man. He was the paragon of his time.

Only a few months before he died in 1987, aged eighty, my wife and I dined with him and his stepdaughter, Chickie, at her Westminster home. It was a delicious evening, with only the four of us present, the last time I saw my old friend alive. After dinner, and fortified with a glass or two of Krug, Henry and I got down to it together. Suddenly (and it wasn't the champagne), he seemed thirty years young again and we were back once more in the great days, the golden days of Waterloo and Ashridge pre-war. All his interest and natural enthusiasm for golf came pouring out in a torrent of thoughts and words. We went through it all and I remember thinking again what a marvellous *talker* he was about the game ... There were the 'rules' he had imparted to his disciples, and the "hitting early from that lovely upright and open position at the top – my trade mark, boy, remember?" Then there were the controversies – "the size of the ball, boy: we were right, weren't we, about that?" And then there was his weak left-hand grip which, pre-war, the Americans had mostly decried.

"Remember what they used to say? 'He'll never last with a weak left hand like that.' Now nearly all of them play showing only two knuckles of the left, or less. Even Ben (Hogan) spent weeks in hospital, after his crash, pulling himself up from his bed with a weak, one knuckle, left-hand grip . . . "

I wouldn't have missed a minute of it . . . Come to that, I wouldn't have missed a page of this book.

PART ONE

Cotton the Man

Chapter 1

*D*uring his later years, in his capacity as legend-in-residence at the Penina Hotel in Portugal, Henry Cotton was often visited by ambitious young professional golfers seeking advice on how to become champions. On those occasions Cotton's attitude was that of an affable monarch receiving supplicants. He dispensed homilies on dress, deportment, diet and courtesy, urging his loyal subjects to avoid junk food, commanding that Ken Brown never enter the dining room again wearing suede boots and stressing the importance of sending thank you letters to everyone who helped them, even to those who could be of no further assistance in their careers.

In this routine of holding court and dispensing wisdom there was a strong family echo from his paternal grandfather, a Cheshire farmer who had a reputation as a rustic Solomon. People came from miles around to put their problems to Farmer Cotton. He would exhort them: "Tell me everything from the beginning and", with a rising inflexion for emphasis, "tell me the truth. Unless you do so I cannot help you." His advice must have been sound because his status as a sage grew with the years, reinforcing the common countryman's view that, while knowledge may be obtained at university, wisdom is best acquired from working with the land.

His son George was disposed to challenge the wisdom of Farmer Cotton's pronouncement: "You are to become a draper." George protested that he had no wish to become a draper. Farmer Cotton's oracular response ended further discussion: "Your wishes are irrelevant in this matter." George was duly indentured to a draper and assigned to the velvet and drapery counter. He shared a room with two other apprentices and spent his evenings in a frenzy of self-improvement, devouring the classics of literature and committing poetry to memory. He had no clear idea of what he wanted to do, except to escape from a lifetime of drudgery as a draper. Neither the verse of Wordsworth nor the prose of Dickens secured his release but his erudition and outgoing personality impressed the ladies who came to the store and often a carriage would be sent to convey him to take tea in the grand house of a wealthy family. His daughter Dorothy believed that these outings were responsible for giving him 'ideas of grandeur far above his station'. In fact the Cottons were no country bumpkins but a solid, county family who could trace their ancestry back to Sir William Cotton who was knighted by Charles II after the restoration of the monarchy and served as MP for Chester for forty years. It was George Cotton's proud boast in later years that he had never once in his life used a public convenience, his habit being to march boldly into the best hotel in the vicinity. His second wife, Alice, was hugely embarrassed when he insisted that she follow the same routine and never overcame her dread that a frock-coated hotel dignitary would discern her purpose and eject her with the admonition that the hotel's amenities were for the exclusive use of the guests.

George Cotton's studious pursuit of knowledge and culture were eventually rewarded by the Wesleyan church. He was made a lay preacher and soon became noted for his spellbinding oratory and for his skill at preparing sermons for the senior ministers of the church. He also developed the capacity, to be inherited by his son Henry, for analysing functions and working out improved ways of performing them. He built up a considerable business manufacturing industrial steam hot-water boilers at Holmes Chapel and by the standards of the day his Victoria Works was a considerable enterprise, big enough to justify its own railway siding. Had he been content to concentrate his full attention and energies on exploiting the opportunities of the industrial revolution there is no telling how the business might have grown. He certainly had the ambition to become a great captain of industry but his lively mind kept diverting him in other directions, another trait inherited by Henry. He became an inventor and built a foundry and workshop onto the family home for his experiments and the construction of prototypes, mainly for agricultural implements such as a potato sorter. He took out more than a dozen patents, all of which were pirated by established manufacturers. He brought actions for these breaches, conducting his own cases, and proved to be a successful advocate, winning one pyrrhic victory after another in the courts. He was, as Dorothy reflected ruefully, an absolute fool with money. In due course much the same judgment was to be made about Henry, by his wife.

While on a trip to Guernsey, where he hoped to sell his patent boiler for heating greenhouses, George Cotton met Alice Le Poidevin who became his second wife and mother to Leslie, Henry and Dorothy. Fortunately for them the Sanderson wall-paper company needed to expand its factory in Holmes Chapel and a good offer was made to George Cotton for the house and the Victoria Works. He accepted and took a job representing the London Salt Company at the invitation of an old Cheshire friend, Henry Seddon, which required him to move to London. The family moved first to Peckham and then to 41 Hawkslade Road, Dulwich, and it was by this chain of events that Henry became a golfer. The boys went to Ivydale Road school, Peckham, then to Reigate grammar school during their evacuation from London during the first world war. George Cotton sold salt in bulk to local authorities and fish markets and at weekends he delighted in listening to the speakers who set up their soap boxes on Peckham Rye. He was a skilled and persistent heckler and counted it a great victory when he exasperated a speaker to the point where he would say: "Here, if you are such a know-all you'd better come up here and have a go yourself." He seized the invitation with alacrity.

He also played golf, with modest skill, owing to an arthritic knee, but enormous enthusiasm. By now he had transferred his own ambitions vicariously to his sons and he decided that they should attend Alleyn's, the public school conveniently near their home. He had a regular salary and for once one of his commercial ventures paid off, albeit modestly. He built a row of twelve garages in Dulwich in anticipation of the motoring boom, reserving one for the family as a golf practice area with a net. He had another net put up in the garden. The family finances could not stretch to covering two lots of fees to Alleyn's and in the typical Cotton family tradition Henry was commanded to win a scholarship. There was a slight logistical problem because Henry was at this time living in Reigate, in Surrey, and the Alleyn's scholarship was by endowment reserved for a boy resident in London. George Cotton used the subterfuge of arranging with his neighbour for Henry's application to be submitted as from 39 Hawkslade Road in order to throw the school off the scent if it should investigate Henry's residential qualifications. Henry duly sat the examination and won the scholarship. Leslie was enrolled as a full fee-paying student. With life returning to normal after the war, George Cotton introduced the boys to golf and when they were aged eight and nine obtained junior memberships for them at the Aquarius club, owned by the Metropolitan Water Board and built on the cover of a south London reservoir. Within three years the boys were so proficient that the club made them full members, an act which would be considered enlightened even today, and both boys won the club championship before reaching their teens. They also showed considerable aptitude for other sports, winning their colours at Alleyn's at football and cricket in teams of boys considerably older than they were.

Even at that early age Henry saw himself as a person apart from the mainstream, highly conscious of his father's dictum: "Always remember that the best is only just good enough for you." Leslie and Dorothy found it difficult to come to terms with Henry's attitude. While they travelled happily on penny trams, Henry insisted on going by taxi. It did not matter to him whether or not he could afford such a luxury; that was the way he had to travel.

In his book *This Game of Golf* Henry claimed that he was a better striker of the golf ball than brother Leslie, sixteen months his senior. Contemporary evidence suggests otherwise. A classmate who played with both of them recalled Leslie as being the superior golfer and cricketer, confirming the wise judgment of the great champion J. H. Taylor. When the boys were aged thirteen and fourteen, George Cotton took both to Taylor for appraisal. Taylor concluded that Leslie was the more gifted player but that Henry was the better prospect because of his superior powers of determination and concentration. A sequence of photographs of Henry's schoolboy swing reveals a curious method, even making due allowances for the fact that he had to freeze the action and hold the pose for the camera at each stage of the swing and that his hand-me-down clubs were so long that he had six inches of grip extending beyond his hands. He treasured those first clubs, keeping the iron heads shiny bright and oiling the hickory shafts, but he later realised that they were monsters. At least he was fortunate in his instinct to grip well down the shaft, unlike some youngsters who start with clubs too long for them. The Japanese champion Isao Aoki, for instance, started playing golf as a young boy with a set of adult clubs which he held at their full length, so that he had to swing them in an extremely flat plane. That idiosyncratic flat swing remained with him for life.

Reflecting on those early days of school and life as young professionals, Leslie recalled how he shared his brother's belief that Henry would make it to the top in whatever sport or profession he chose. He himself had little in the way of a competitive spirit and suppressed what he had, so he felt, because he was the elder brother. He had to 'take it easy' against Henry because of the difference in their sizes and ages whereas Henry had to exert himself to the limit. By nature Leslie was easy going and his real ambition was to become a professional musician. If he was rather reluctantly pushed into becoming a golf professional, he developed into a very good one, both as a player and a teacher. But good golf, hitting the ball straight up the fairway, bored him and, lacking ambition for conquest and results, he maintained his interest by experimenting with unnecessary fades and hooks. He hit shots for their own sake rather than for the basic purpose of scoring as well as possible. His satisfactions from golf came from people and helping them with their games. Golf was his work and music was his pleasure, complementary activities in his view since rhythm is the basis of good golf and the breath control for playing a trumpet is excellent exercise for an athlete. He was immensely proud of Henry's progress which he followed avidly with no trace of envy, although from a distance because he spent most of his career working in South Africa, where he died in 1987.

Henry's conviction that he was especially favoured by fate was manifested by a rebellious nature which was to change the entire direction of his life. At Alleyn's he planned to go on to university and graduate as a civil engineer, a profession he thought would give him a comfortable living and enable him to play amateur golf and cricket for his beloved Surrey. This plan was in no way compromised by his first experience of top-level amateur golf when he was disqualified in the Boys' Championship of 1921 for grounding his golf bag in a hazard, an infringement since eliminated from the game's criminal code.

Leslie had left Alleyn's at the age of seventeen for he had no academic ambitions or qualifications. George Cotton had arranged for him to go as an assistant to George Oke at Fulwell. Oke was well known to the family because he had been professional at the Honor Oak and Forest Hill golf club while George Cotton had been a member and where he and the boys had played many times. So Cotton Minor had lost his distinguishing suffix by the time of the fateful day when Alleyn's first XI played an away match at Marlow. The incident is worth recording in detail because it illuminates in its stark, juvenile expression a side of Henry's character which was to govern his career although decently shrouded in an overlay of sophistication.

The team travelled by public transport in those days and the senior members had arranged to take some girls out on the river after the match. This romantic tryst meant that the four juniors had to take the team's cricket bag as well as their own bags back to Dulwich by themselves. On the train they composed a note in the following terms:

> We the undersigned beg to show our kind appreciation of being allowed the privilege of transporting the cricket bag from Marlow to Dulwich to the detriment of our tender muscles and to the advantage of the select and most condescending. We were surprised to find the bag taken as far as the station. We think it is a pity that people who are supposed to be looked up to for example should so fail in their thoughts for the school and their fellow beings.
>
> Signed: E. Bailey, L. A. Coles, T. H. Cotton, L. A. Vigurs

This note was pushed under the door of the prefects' room and its discovery caused an explosion of righteous indignation among the prefects and masters. What effrontery for juniors to lecture their elders and betters on sportsmanship and natural justice. The following Thursday the four miscreants were summoned to the prefects' room. T. H. Cotton was commanded to enter first. He refused, on the grounds that they had determined to stand together. The captain of the school replied that in that case they would have to go before the headmaster, R. B. Henderson. The prefects reluctantly agreed to the headmaster's request that the four boys should be taken together. In an account written at the time at the request of his father, Henry wrote that resistance was useless against a gathering of about forty prefects and that his three friends were in turn 'brutally, vindictively and excessively thrashed by four school prefects with canes (including one walking cane). The prefects struck with all their might and were particularly vicious.' He himself refused to be caned on medical grounds and was commanded to produce a medical certificate or suffer the same, or worse, treatment. George Cotton was outraged. His first instinct was to withdraw Henry from the school immediately. His second thought was to fire off a letter to the headmaster:

> Dear Sir, I much regret having to write to you on such a subject. I had hoped that we had progressed far beyond such vindictive and brutal proceedings. However, such is not the case. I therefore appeal to you as Headmaster to supply forthwith the answers to the following questions, A, B and C.
>
> A. What has my son done wrong?
> B. What corporal punishment did you authorise?
> C. What persons did you authorise to carry it out?
>
> On looking over my boy's reports for the last four and a half years I cannot conceive him to be guilty of any serious crime, hence I feel it my painful duty to take the necessary steps to protect my boy and therefore I appeal to you for protection for my son against repetition of assaults the prefects committed upon him last week and against any victimisation of any kind whatsoever.
>
> I take a very serious view of the events of last week. Quite apart from the physical torture inflicted upon three cricket colleagues witnessed by my son there is the serious injury, loss and damage he suffers to character, reputation and prospects. Under all the circumstances your early answers to the questions herein will enable me to decide upon my course of action and promptly deal with it as far as my son is concerned.
>
> Yours respectfully,
> George Cotton

With commendable restraint, the headmaster replied:

> I understand that your son did not receive any punishment at the hands of the prefects or in any other way for his offence last week. I am therefore a little at a loss to understand precisely what is the cause of your complaint. Your son has pleaded 'medical unfitness' and though no evidence has yet been produced in support of this contention he is being treated in accordance with his own contention.

Such soft words did nothing to turn away the wrath of George Cotton. A doctor who was a member of the same golf club was prevailed upon to certify that Henry's state of health was such that corporal punishment as threatened was inadvisable. The parents of the three boys who had been caned saw in George Cotton a doughty champion for boys' rights in a school which had earned a reputation, at least among the victims, for excessive and particularly brutal physical punishments. Other parents whose boys had been caned joined in a council of war at the Cotton home. The upshot was a parents' meeting at the school, addressed by the headmaster.

George Cotton followed his usual tactic of sitting at the back of the hall and making whispered asides to those around him. With the deep sarcasm without which it is apparently impossible to be a teacher at an English public school, R. B. Henderson called out: "You at the back. Instead of muttering to your friends why don't you come up onto the platform and give us all the benefit of your wisdom." The old Peckham Rye ploy had worked exactly as planned. George Cotton's practised oratory soon had the audience in thrall. He whipped the parents into such a frenzy of indignation that when an over-wrought father jumped up and proposed that Henderson be sacked the meeting carried the resolution by acclamation. Things had clearly gone too far.

In the days that followed, and in the lowered temperature of private discussions, a deal was done. A parents' committee would be formed to hear grievances and to act as liaison body with the school authorities.

George Cotton was not finished yet, however. He wrote to the headmaster:

> I herein enclose the medical certificate to prove my son's contention and much regret that you have not carried out your promise not to victimise, threaten or insult my son further over this matter of discipline. I protested to you at the meeting of parents against boys flogging boys cruelly and vindictively for minor offences or any offence whatsoever. The alleged offence does not merit any punishment at all.

The next day the headmaster received another broadside:

> My son informs me that you summoned him to your room yesterday and that he refused your request to be flogged by the

prefects. You then threatened to injure him by reporting him (a scholarship boy) to the County Council. In this case the punishment would not fit the crime.

That letter was accompanied by an apology from Henry: "I, T. H. Cotton, hereby tender my sincere apology to R. B. Henderson Esq., Headmaster of Alleyn's school, and to the prefects of Alleyn's school for any offence contained in the note bearing my signature of the 19th inst."

The olive branch was swiftly followed by another dart:

On careful deliberation upon my son's best interests and also the welfare of the school I herein request you kindly to allow him to devote the few remaining weeks of the term entirely to his studies. I therefore desire his entire withdrawal from all cricket as you informed him that his further connection with the cricket teams was not desired.

The headmaster was in no mood to accept any proposal from George Cotton and replied:

Nothing would be easier than for me to accede to your request. In fact I cannot help a feeling that it would be too easy. I have set myself the task of finding a means of reconciliation between your boy and his fellows and to adopt your plan would simply mean an abandonment of a very difficult task. Moreover such an action on the part of the boy at this time would be in grave danger of misconstruction. Others would, I fear, jump to the conclusion that your son preferred playing golf for himself to playing cricket for the school. Of course this could not be true but it is important to avoid all possible grounds of misunder-standing. It is, unhappily, quite true that at present his fellows do not want him but I have by no means given up hope of breaking down this barrier and restoring better relations. It is a terrible thing for the boy to have this cloud over him and I want to dispel it. If you will trust me and support any action I find necessary I believe we can win.

That trust and support were not forthcoming. The father of one of the caned boys instructed his solicitor to compile a full account of the saga, including a medical report on the state of his son's buttocks signed by the same doctor who certified Henry as being in no state of health for corporal punishment, and this was sent to the governors of Alleyn's. The practice of canings by prefects was subsequently discontinued.

The impasse over Henry would be resolved by his leaving the school. There was no suggestion of his being expelled, but equally there was no doubt that he could not remain at Alleyn's. The breach was made with mutual relief. Henry was glad to be free of a regime which had become intolerable to him; the school was equally glad to be free of the interference and gratuitous advice, particularly in matters of the cricket and football teams, from George Cotton. So Henry left and at the age of sixteen became a golf professional, thereby forfeiting his right to a Christian name under the contemporary conventions of sport. In like spirit, he will become plain Cotton for the remainder of this account.

Chapter 2

*C*otton's decision, abetted by his father, to become a golf professional at the age of sixteen would be unremarkable these days when a successful tournament professional can become a millionaire by the age of twenty-five and be fêted as a demi-god and invited to dine at Buckingham Palace. In the twenties, when the lines of class distinction were closely drawn, the game offered no prospects of fortune or social advancement. Golf was a pastime for the well-to-do upper and middle classes and their clubs were bastions of privilege. Cotton was deliberately turning his back on that world and relegating himself to the status of a servant, and the lowest grade of kitchen boy at that.

The head professional at a golf club in those days was regarded as a sergeant-major figure. Within his own domain of the shop he was a lordly figure whose authority over the ranks of assistant professionals was absolute. But he in turn was at the beck and call of the most junior member and he would not dream of entering the clubhouse unless invited by a member. When he went away to play a championship he changed in the shop of the home professional, a simple process involving only replacing his shoes with the tackety (hobnailed) boots favoured for golf. The championships had to be completed by Friday evening so that the professionals could return to their clubs in time to play with the captain at weekends.

The professionals knew their place. In their wildest imaginings they could not have dreamt that one day fleets of courtesy cars would meet them, sweep them off to luxury suites in the best hotels, call for them in the morning to convey them to the course where they would be treated like visiting royalty with their own lounges, crèches for their children, and that the members would happily vacate the locker room for their benefit. It is true that at this period the American professional Walter Hagen was beginning to challenge the established order but he was regarded as an upstart and, being an American, someone who knew no better. Cotton was later to say of Hagen: "He lived like a prince and was treated like one. Pros today should go down on their knees and say a prayer of thanks for what he did for our profession."

Cotton obtained a position as the junior of six assistants to George Oke at Fulwell golf club at 12s 6d a week. Leslie had also started with Oke and had since moved on. As the lowest in the hierarchy of dogsbodies Henry had the worst of the menial jobs in the shop, sweeping the floor, cleaning shoes and clubs and sand-papering hickory shafts for the clubmaker. This last task was considered to be the hardest and most soul-destroying chore an apprentice could be given but Cotton was grateful for it. His understanding of the mechanics of golf was minimal but instinctively he felt that strong hands and arms were of paramount importance to the proper playing of the game. He regarded his long hours of sand-papering as a training exercise, spent his lunch break practising his golf and when finally the last member had left the club and he was able to lock up shop he hurried back to the family home in Dulwich and hit hundreds of shots into the net in the garage.

By embracing this new life he had committed an act of social treason, thoroughly letting down the side by the standards of his former friends at Alleyn's. But Cotton reasoned that just as they had rejected him, so he rejected them and their values. He had his vision and, since the world of golf he had entered also regarded him as an outsider, he would have to make his way alone. This feeling of being an outcast sustained him through the drudgery of his early apprenticeship and increased his determination for success.

His progress as a player might have been accelerated at this period if he had been content to fit into the system and follow the instruction of Oke who was a highly competent player and teacher. Conventional wisdom insisted that golf should be played with a stiff left arm guiding and controlling the stroke. The lonely rebel rejected that doctrine. The right hand was the stronger and logic insisted that its power must be employed to the full. He preferred to seek his own salvation through trial and error. Cotton was deeply unpopular among the other assistants who regarded him as arrogant and stand-offish.

After nine months at Fulwell, Cotton answered an advertisement for an assistant's post at Rye on the Sussex coast and was taken on by Alex Simpson who had been severely wounded in the hip while serving with the Black Watch during the war. The wound gave him severe pain and badly restricted his walking. This was an idyllic period for Cotton. As sixth assistant at Fulwell he was very seldom called upon to play with a member; as the only assistant at Rye the opportunities were plentiful. Apart from indulging his golfing passion, the playing made him known to men of influence who could help him in his career.

One of his daily chores was to fetch the milk from a farm which lay on the far side of the golf course. Cotton turned the chore into a pleasant diversion by taking a club with him and playing his way over an ad hoc course across the fields to the farm. This exercise improved his golf and in later years he encouraged his pupils to play occasional rounds of golf using only one club in order to teach them to improvise shots and manipulate the ball with their hands.

One of the members with whom Cotton played at Rye was Major Cyril Tolley MC who, along with Roger Wethered, dominated amateur golf. At that period there was no incentive for amateurs to turn professional and the leading amateurs were a match for the pros. Tolley, a bachelor of independent means and twelve years Cotton's senior, was a formidable golfer who had already won the first of his two Amateur championships. He was a mighty hitter and drove the green of the 350-yard first hole at Troon in the 1923 Open and twice drove the 370-yard eighteenth hole at St Andrews during the Jubilee Vase of 1927. Tolley arranged for Cotton to take an appointment as playing assistant for the winter season at Mougins on the French Riviera, the first time that his educational background had proved an asset in his new career since he had won a special credit for oral French in his school certificate examination. The venture did not last long. Before the season was over Cotton wired his father for the fare home, complaining of gastric poisoning.

By this time Cotton had qualified for full membership of the Professional Golfers' Association, enabling him to play in the few tournaments that were organised at that time. Through the influence of his good friend Tolley, who had also taken him to Prestwick to play in his first Open championship, Cotton was shortlisted for the job of head professional at Langley Park close to the family home at Dulwich. The letter informing him of this development read as follows:

> The committee has considered various applications for the post of professional to this club and your name is on the selected list. The terms offered are £2 10s per week retaining fee (you to employ a competent assistant) with sale of clubs, balls etc and fees for playing and teaching. If these are of interest to you the committee would be glad of an interview with you on Thursday next at 5 p.m. here. Your references state nothing about your capability as a clubmaker and the committee would be glad of further information on that point if you will bring references with you.

In his reply Cotton detailed his training in club repair and added that he had done nearly all the clubmaking at Rye and had made clubs for several leading players including Mr C. J. H. Tolley. This was a slightly exaggerated claim because the lame Alex Simpson had occupied himself mainly at the clubmaker's bench while Cotton played golf with the members but he was a competent enough craftsman and took some samples of his work with him to the interview. The following day the secretary of Langley Park wrote with the news that the committee had decided to appoint him as the club professional. In addition to his retainer of £2 10s a week, the terms included the following scale of charges: Playing, 5s a round. Lessons, 4s per hour and 2s 6d per half hour. He would be permitted forty-two days a year absence from the club for playing competitions.

At the age of nineteen years and three months Cotton had achieved his first distinction as the youngest golfer ever to be appointed as head professional in the history of British golf. His youth gave rise to some misgivings in one of the elder statesmen at his previous club who wrote to him:

> If, as an older man, I may venture a little advice I would say that respect and politeness are never thrown away on your elders while the lack of them is quickly noted against a man, and that steadiness of character, especially with regard to liquor and

women, is the greatest asset a man can have when he applies for a responsible job.

This homily was superfluous. Cotton neither smoked nor drank, although he was later ordered by his doctor to follow the wise advice of St Paul and take a little wine for his stomach's sake. And he couldn't be bothered with women at this period, in the recollection of Walter Hitchcock who knew him well and was himself later to become head professional at Langley Park. Golf was Cotton's jealous and demanding mistress. Hitchcock, son of the club's greenkeeper, was deeply impressed and rather shocked by the arrogant bearing of the youth who commanded the club steward to prepare special meals for him and who forced himself to walk in the address position, pigeon-toed and with a dropped right shoulder. Hitchcock even tried to copy that posture in the hope that he might emulate Cotton's immaculate striking. "I saw them all and I don't think anyone hit the ball better," he recalled. Being of the old school, Hitchcock did not try to copy Cotton's imperious manner, such as his reaction when another professional came to Langley to play and, in the usual custom, changed his shoes in the shop. When Cotton returned from lunch and saw the shoes he picked them up and hurled them across the car park.

Although he was still subject to the traditional constraints implicit in the job of a club professional, Cotton now controlled his own fate as a player and was able to practise as much as he liked, as well as put his instructional theories into practice on the pupils. His ambition drove him to practise for inordinate lengths of time. Most days he did not impose on the steward for a special meal and lunch consisted of a biscuit and chocolate bar. On the putting green he would ring one of the holes with balls and putt for hours. He found it easier to stay in the crouched position rather than stand erect between putts and on occasions at the end of these marathon sessions he was unable to stand up and had to be carried off the green bent double. To strengthen his hands he continued his schoolboy routine of scything through rough grass with a club and often his hands were bleeding when he cycled home to Dulwich in the evenings. Then he would continue hitting balls in the garage. He ignored warnings that he was trying to do too much although he later conceded that his health was damaged by these obsessive labours. The truth is that he could not bring himself to slow down because he was the victim of demonic possession: success was not just something he wanted, he needed it to survive.

When he could no longer ignore the damage he was doing to himself he eased his physical burden of an arduous train and bicycle journey to work from Dulwich by setting himself up in a bachelor pad near the club. He bought a church hall, St Mary's Hall, Bromley, and had the word 'Hall' obliterated. An architect was engaged to convert it into a suitable dwelling with, at Cotton's insistence, a most lavish bathroom. His old nanny became his housekeeper. By this time Cotton was beginning to attract the interest of equipment manufacturers and the chairman of Spaldings went to lunch at St Mary's. "Henry had a unique living room," he recalled, "furnished with low coffee tables and at least one hundred cushions, which you were supposed to pile up against the wall. We went in there for coffee after lunch and it was so surprisingly comfortable that I all but fell asleep before the coffee came."

By this time Britain's traditional supremacy in golf had been firmly surpassed by the United States. After some earlier false starts the game took root in America towards the end of the nineteenth century and up until the first world war professional golf was dominated by immigrant Scottish players. Native Americans then took up the running as the craze for golf gripped the nation and the new breed of home-bred professionals, uninhibited by social constrictions, elevated both the standing and the standards of their calling. A structured calendar of regular tournaments persuaded the best of them to specialise as tournament players, without benefit of a golf club appointment, and this development provided a powerful stimulus to advances in technique since they had to play well in order to survive. Cotton was strongly attracted by this development and he knew that if he was ever to become a world beater he must play with, and learn from, the best players in the world. With the blessing of the Langley Park committee and members he put all his resources into a £300 letter of credit and a ticket – first class of course – on the *Aquitania*, and sailed for America to compete in the winter session of 1928-29.

All those hours of hitting golf balls into a net in the restricted space of the family garage had given him a markedly upright swing which hit the ball in a curving flight pattern from left to right, a fade. It was a style which enabled him to control his shots and keep out of trouble but it meant he must pay for his accuracy with a considerable loss of distance. The American power game was a revelation to him. They had the advantage that by this time steel golf shafts had been legalised in America which meant that they could practise as long and hard as they liked whereas Cotton, like all hickory shaft players, had to be extremely careful to guard against breaking his brittle shafts through overuse.

The other, even more pertinent, difference was that the Americans out-drove him by considerable distances because they hit the ball with a right to left flight, or draw, which made the ball run a long way after pitching on the fairway. As a result Cotton found that he had to use a fairway wood club for his second shots on holes where his rivals were playing mid-irons to the green. Even so, he finished third for a prize of £80 in his first tournament. The young Englishman was made very welcome by the American players and he benefited from one of the conventions of the gentleman's game that professionals are always ready with help and advice for other professionals. Two players in particular were generous with wise counsel, the West Virginian hillbilly Sam Snead and the expatriate Scot, Tommy Armour. Both urged him to change his technique so that he could hit the ball with draw and profit from the extra length of drive.

This may not sound too drastic to a non-golfer. In fact, for a professional golfer who has hit hundreds of balls a day for years in a certain style the action becomes habituated and the muscles employed in that swing are so conditioned that even the smallest change in technique takes months, or years in some cases such as Nick Faldo, to accomplish. The muscles used in the old swing have to become dormant and a new combination of muscles has to be developed. Since golfers at this level concentrate on where they are going to hit the ball, rather than how they are going to make the stroke, there is an overwhelming tendency during the transitional period for the body to revert to the old method of its own volition.

Cotton worked hard on making the necessary adjustments and he was greatly heartened in his labours by the arrival of a telegram from the Professional Golfers' Association informing him that he had been nominated as one of the ten players from which the eight-man team would be selected for the Ryder Cup match, to be played against the United States the following April at

Moortown. The full invitation which followed stressed: "The maximum allowance for expenses is fixed at £3 10s per day to include all railway fares and a statement of expenditure must accompany your application for refund of expenses incurred."

Cotton's association with the leading American players on this visit had given him a clear appreciation of the task the British and Irish team would face at Moortown and reinforced his determination to be worthy of the challenge. During the rest of his trip Cotton made little impact in the tournaments, not that he had any extravagant expectations. He had always seen this expedition as a learning experience and when he returned home in March 1929, he counted himself as having been immeasurably enriched. He had acquired a new and much more effective technique, a lasting love and admiration for America, a taste for colourful and comfortable golf dress, and his letter of credit for £300 was still intact.

Cotton had attracted considerable press attention from the time he turned professional at the age of sixteen. He was a novelty and it became almost obligatory to refer to him as 'the public school golfer', just as Fleet Street felt compelled to tack labels onto surgeons, who were invariably 'eminent' and Roman Catholics who were unfailingly 'devout'. The rich promise of the public school golfer had been recognised by the more discerning writers, mainly because of his obvious courage, determination and hard work. The Ryder Cup match provided scope for a new cliché. Cotton became the 'babe of the team' but when he secured the winning point for Great Britain by beating Al Watrous in the singles, all that changed. He was now an established player in his own right, without benefit of the public school trimmings.

The success in the Ryder Cup bred further triumphs and more opportunities in commerce and journalism. The *Evening News* engaged him to write a weekly column on golf and he appeared in large advertisements extolling the virtues of Yeast-Vite tablets. ("I always like to take two or three tablets before entering an important golf tournament or match. In fact, I am now trying a real course of Yeast-Vite tablets and have already derived great benefit.") He was engaged to complete a team of six leading golfers, including the great champions, Harry Vardon, Ted Ray and J. H. Taylor, for a golf week at Gamages store, giving lessons and advice in the sports department which had been fitted with a real bunker, putting green and driving net. Cotton took the opportunity to push the sales of Cotton-Oxford golf shoes.

This enterprise was such a success that the same team was engaged for a similar golf week at Barkers store. Vardon was an old hand at this kind of thing. In 1900 on a promotional tour of the United States this legendary player, who was to win a record six Open championships, was engaged to demonstrate his genius by hitting balls into a net at the Jordan-Marsh department store in Boston. He became so bored by what he considered to be a pointless exercise that he amused himself by aiming at the tiny valve of a fire extinguisher which projected through the net. Vardon hit this minute target so frequently that the manager begged him to desist for fear that he might flood the place.

While Cotton was now firmly established as a force in British golf he was by no means a popular figure. The older champions such as the men he had joined for the department store golf weeks understood his ambitions for himself and the profession and were supportive. J. H. Taylor in particular shared his vision of raising the status and rewards of the professional golfer and had been the prime mover in the formation of the Professional Golfers' Association. But the players of his own generation considered him to be aloof, snobbish, selfish and ostentatious with his flashy style of dress. These attitudes may have been fuelled by jealousy for his enterprise in exploiting his success through journalism and commercial deals and partly because he was upsetting the established order. Like other reforming pioneers before him, his motives were misconstrued, an example being his decision not to enter for the Kent professional championship after winning it five times in succession. It was assumed that he felt it beneath him to support his county association once he had achieved prominence in the game. In fact, Cotton stopped entering the championship in order to give someone else a chance to win it and perhaps be inspired to go on to greater things.

For the first time in their careers as professionals, Cotton teamed up with his brother, Leslie, for the Midland Open Foursomes at Gerrards Cross. They won by a stroke from the experienced Ryder Cup brothers, Charles and Ernest Whitcombe. The anonymous (but unmistakably Bernard Darwin) golf correspondent of *The Times* wrote:

It was Henry who, in this instance, took control of the partnership and piloted it to success, though occasionally I could not help thinking that if the advice had been less frequent Leslie would have made fewer major errors, and the margin of victory would have been more convincing. The art of foursomes play is to have implicit faith in your partner, and to offer advice only when it is asked. Advice given in any other circumstances is calculated to disturb your partner by getting him into two minds, a condition of things which is fatal to a well-ordered understanding.

The anti-Cotton feelings among the professionals seeped into the press, good-naturedly enough in the cartoons of Tom Webster and others but with a sharp critical edge among the writers. Cotton was therefore in a receptive frame of mind when he received an invitation to visit Argentina the following winter in the company of Aubrey Boomer to give lessons and play exhibitions. Boomer and his twin brother both held club appointments on the continent and this was to be a factor in Cotton's destiny, following the long sea voyage to Buenos Aires when there was little to do except chat to each other. Cotton had already had a glimpse of the possibilities in France for an enterprising golf professional who spoke the language fluently. Boomer enlarged on those possibilities. But they were sailing towards someone else who was to have a far greater impact on the life and career of T. H. Cotton.

Chapter 3

*T*he enthusiastic patronage of the Stuart kings, inevitably echoed by the aristocracy, and the sheer expense of a game involving a ball costing a labourer's weekly wage (and which might be demolished by one careless stroke) gave golf a fashionable cachet which lingered down the centuries. Such was the social aura of the game in the eighteenth century that golf clubs were formed in the United States which had no courses and members who had no intention of taking up the game. It just happened to be the done thing to be a member of a golf club. The Mar del Plata club near Buenos Aires also had a large number of members who did not play golf but who had joined the club for social reasons and to enjoy the ancillary amenities such as the restaurant, hairdressing salons and massage parlours. These social members could have no idea of who Henry Cotton might be so the club prepared the way as best it could in order that the famous visiting sportsmen would be welcomed with due honour.

Having stimulated an interest in the approaching golf festival among the social members, the club invited members to book lessons from the great professionals. These lessons were paid for in advance so there was a guaranteed source of revenue waiting for Cotton and Boomer. Cotton therefore scanned the list with interest on arrival at the club and any disappointment he may have felt at the fact that Boomer had attracted the most pupils was dispelled by the intriguing paradox that his own allotment of teaching engagements was also entirely full. A closer inspection of the list revealed the reason. A Señora Isabel-Maria Estanguet de Moss had booked a course of fifty lessons. He did not know then that she had booked with Cotton only because Boomer's list had been full when she went to add her name.

On the same notice-board was a display of photographs taken at a recent club function which the members could order. One of them was of Señora Moss, and Cotton bought it. Cotton was very conscious of his matinée idol good looks and the care he took over his appearance owed as much to vanity as his professional instincts to dress the part of the champion he was determined to become. He was flattered by that commitment to fifty lessons and misinterpreted it to mean that he had made a conquest.

The photograph did not entirely prepare him for the tiny, pert figure who strode purposefully down the path to the teaching area. No camera ever did justice to Isabel Moss. She was no classical beauty; her high cheek bones hinted at Aztec blood in her genetic cocktail and the prominent front teeth, while adding an extra luminance to her smile, gave her a severe, school marm expression when she sheathed them, with difficulty, with her lips. Yet she was undeniably and dramatically attractive. She radiated an electric field of vivacity. You could not see it but you could not fail to detect it. Central Casting would have immediately tagged her as Latin Bombshell type.

The first lesson was not a success. Cotton, who believed that the only way to make a woman do something was to say that it was beyond her capabilities, told her that she was wasting her money and would never make a golfer. She snapped back that he was the most insufferable man she had ever met. It was, in short, love at first sight. Years later when questioned about their first meeting she would amuse dinner-party guests by saying: "I fell in love with his golf." Cotton, who in defence of his self-esteem had acquired a useful verbal counter-punch, responded: "And I fell in love with her money." Throughout the half-century and more they were to spend together they maintained in public a façade of antagonism, exchanging verbal darts which those who did not know them well took to be the genuine crossfire of combatants in the war between the sexes. This may have started as a smoke-screen before they were married, to conceal their mutual affection and stop the wagging of gossiping tongues, acting as a lid on the boiling cauldron of their true feelings.

There was, in truth, an extremely lovable amount of money attached to the woman the golfing community came to know as 'Toots'. Her father owned the biggest *estancia* in Argentina. When

Cotton was taken to see it on that visit he was incredulous. It was, he recalled, like going to somewhere the size of Wales and being told: "This is our place in the country."

The family home in the most fashionable avenue of Buenos Aires was called the Petit Hôtel Sante Fe 1681. It was not petit or an hotel, more like a smallish palace. Until now Cotton's adult life had been golf, golf and golf. He had no other interest and was an innocent about the finer things of life. This trip to Argentina was a revelation as it was borne in on him that golf might be more than an end in itself; it might be a means to an end. The beef baron's daughter who was five years his senior had made a good marriage, to Enrique Moss, a high flyer in the Argentine diplomatic service whose younger brother was a noted racing driver and darling of Buenos Aires society. Roles became reversed, with Cotton the avid pupil and the Mosses his tutors. He needed no instruction in the appreciation of obvious beauty, such as the marble statues of naked maidens being importuned by cherubs which adorned recesses in the Petit Hôtel. This, he realised, was the world he wanted to inherit and he was eager to learn how to identify a Louis XIV commode, how to discourse on the old masters and how to select a fine wine.

The two professionals had a punishing programme on this trip. They taught from 8 a.m. until dark and played exhibition matches against local professionals at weekends. In addition, Cotton had to find time to write articles for five different newspapers each week. He became thoroughly run down and came out in boils. The Mosses nursed him back to health and in partnership with Boomer he won a match which was billed as Britain versus Argentina against two of the country's leading golfers and then won the Mar del Plata Open championship.

Cotton's return to Langley Park and the humdrum life of a club professional reinforced his determination to make good. Most young professionals start off with their goals firmly orientated on money and it is not until they have achieved a measure of financial independence that they begin to concentrate their ambitions on the honours of the game. Cotton, like the American champion, Jack Nicklaus, realised right from the beginning that if he concentrated on winning the major honours then the rewards would follow automatically.

Representing your country is an undoubted honour and the nation's golf fans looked forward to Cotton repeating his Ryder

Cup success in the team which was due to sail to America in 1931 to play the Americans. Cotton had just won his really big tournament at Southport, beating a strong field of domestic and overseas players including four members of the American Ryder Cup team, to confirm his standing as the best young player in Britain. The news, announced within an hour of the end of that tournament, that he had been excluded from the team was a sensation.

Members of the team were subject to certain conditions, one of which was that the team would return to Britain together after the match. When he had been approached and asked if he was available for selection, Cotton had replied that he would be only too happy to play if he could remain in the United States after the match so that he could play some tournaments on the American circuit. He issued a public statement to that effect. Ironically, the chairman of the PGA was his old boss, George Oke, who reported this exchange back to the committee. A statement was issued saying that exceptions to the match conditions could not be made for individuals. Once again Cotton found himself at loggerheads with authority, only this time it was not only the prefects of the PGA but the whole country who wanted to cane him.

Behind the scenes there was much diplomatic activity in an attempt to resolve the problem. The root cause of this situation was a conflict which was to bedevil Ryder Cup selection for years to come: whether selection to the team was to be an honour conferred by the Professional Golfers' Association for loyal and meritorious service or whether it should be a process of choosing the team most likely to win the trophy. Already two obvious candidates, Percy Alliss and Aubrey Boomer, had been ruled out of consideration because they were based on the continent. Without Cotton, Britain would be sending a team lacking three of its finest golfers. Cotton was given to understand through unofficial channels that if he would apologise to the PGA all might be well. He replied that he could do no such thing because he had nothing to apologise for. The PGA then received a message on the bush telegraph to the effect that Cotton might be disposed to respond favourably if he received a formal invitation to play. Oke approached him to discuss this possibility. Cotton asked if the same condition about returning home with the team still applied. Oke confirmed that this was the case. Cotton said that since the original announcement about his exclusion from the team he had made so many engagements that he simply could not fulfil them if he had to return with the team. The PGA then announced that Bert Hodson of Chigwell had been chosen to fill the last vacancy. A British team averaging nearly forty years of age then sailed off to Columbus, Ohio, accompanied by Cotton in his capacity as a newspaper reporter, and was soundly thrashed. Cotton the anti-hero was widely regarded as having added treason to his charge sheet.

His close friends were worried about his negative image. And when Cotton also declined to play for England against Scotland, on the grounds that the match was to be played two days before the Open championship when the players should be concentrating on stroke-play, the editor of *Golf Illustrated*, Eliot Cockel, who enjoyed a close relationship with his celebrated columnist, wrote him a long letter. In part it read:

So far as I see the position it is this: The PGA feels that you enjoy the various benefits that accrue to its members, such as the ability to play, and in your case to win, their various valuable tournaments. But when they want you to do something for them such as representing England against Scotland, you reply: "Nothing doing; it does not suit my book." They therefore feel that whilst you are prepared to accept the various benefits you are not prepared to shoulder certain moral responsibilities.

I think this letter you have received [from the PGA] is the culmination of your attitude to the Ryder Cup last year, with which I entirely concurred and still sympathise. That attitude, by being followed up by your refusal to play for England this year, has got them on the raw. Whilst I fully understand why you did not wish to play, had I been at Southport I would not have advised you to have issued the public communiqué that you did. I would sooner have gone to the PGA committee and explained to them that you were not in good health and have asked them to let you off and I am sure they would have done.

The above is roughly the position and there are two courses open. (1) To reply to the PGA and ask them to put out in detail the various grievances they have against you, or (2) to acknowledge their letter simply saying that you have not intended to avoid your moral obligations. Whichever step you take I shall be only too pleased as you know to draft a suitable letter for you. I suggest this because I think a time has come for diplomatic relations. You must remember that the PGA can make any rule it pleases and if the committee decided to chuck you out I feel that you would be the loser. It would bar you from participating in practically every tournament in this country except the Open.

To this you may say "What will be the attitude of the public?" Now Henry I want to be frank with you and I know you will take it from me as a pal. At the moment you are not popular with the public. You may turn around and say to me that you always get the crowd. That is true enough but don't forget that the crowd will very often follow a great exponent of any art at the same time disliking him and wishing him ill.

You have always been an individualist and I am a believer in individualism, but I do not think I would be advising you right if I did not warn you that individualism can be carried to such a point that it estranges the friendship of the public. I want you to reflect what your popularity with the public means. It is the basis upon which all your exhibition games are founded. It is the basis upon which all your writing is founded. It is quite possible for the public to say about a man, "I know he knows all about this game, but I dislike him so much that I am not going to read him." If that comes about your value as a writer drops.

I now want to touch upon a very personal matter and again I would ask you to believe that I can only do so because I feel that you and I are something more to each other than merely money-making machines. I personally do not care a damn about how you dress. I know you, and I like that part of you that has nothing to do with your outer garb. But you are a public figure and a Britisher, and the British public is proud of the fact that you are a Britisher. Therefore can you understand public feeling if they see you in a foreign garb? They tack this on to the fact that you refused to play for Britain against America and for England against Scotland, and they jump to the conclusion that you are denying the country of your origin. And they do not like it. They read into it a hostile act on your part.

Believe me there is a feeling amongst the golf public that you are high-hatting them. [This expression was clearly chosen deliberately because Cotton had been much ridiculed for playing in a wide-brimmed caballero hat he had brought home from Argentina.] I do not think this is an attitude that pays in the long run. Archie Compston was inclined to high-hat them at one time. He got the publicity all right, but I do not think it was the right sort of publicity. Walter Hagen was another who was inclined to be high-hatted at one time. It is all very well to say that so long as you keep winning you retain your money-making power. That is true enough, but there comes a time in the life of every artiste when he or she cannot connect with success, and it is at such times that the value of popularity stands them in good stead. When you have a streak when you cannot win it is the popularity you have built up whilst you were winning that keeps you going and helps you to get back.

The cleverest handler of the public that this game has ever known was Bob Jones (the American amateur who dominated the great championships in the twenties, beating the finest professionals in achieving the grand slam of golf). You know that I know Bob very well and I couldn't count the times that Bob has laughed to me after one of his speeches about such and such a course being the greatest he had ever played and such and such a public being the most wonderful that had ever graced a performance. In private he would tell me that the course was lousy and the public who had followed him lousier still! But that soft soap brought him to a position where he was worshipped and now that he has gone out of first class play that astonishing popularity is bringing him in thousands of pounds.

You have been too outspoken in both manner and speech. I know it is damned annoying when someone comes and asks you silly questions in the middle of a championship round, but it is as possible to choke them off nicely as it is to tell them to go to hell. If you do it nicely they say "Henry Cotton is a fine fellow", but if you do it nastily they say "There goes that four-letter person." And he goes along and tells his pals and his pals add a bit and tell their pals and gradually there is a whole lot of people getting a wrong view of you.

[...]

I believe in individualism but I think we must control it, and I do honestly think that you have taken your individualism far enough for the time being. You have established yourself as a character and I would be inclined to spend the next year or two in consolidating that position and by your actions, manner and speech leading the public to believe that they have misjudged you. If you can reach that position you can become more of an individualist than ever, and the public will take it from you

35

whilst at the moment they are inclined to resent it. I feel sure you will read this letter as an expression of a pal to a pal and that if you do not understand it you will come and talk to me about it. After all the public that you and I serve is the same and I have known it for twenty years longer than you have. Finally, it is deucedly difficult to give of your best before a hostile crowd. You may succeed but it takes so much out of you and it seems a pity to waste that extra energy.

Cotton pondered the implications of these home truths and the irony that no man is a prophet in his own country. Was it equally true, he wondered, that absence really did make the heart grow fonder? He had personal experience of the phenomenon since returning home in his feelings towards Toots. He was in no mood to change his ways, since he felt that his successes in golf were the result of his policy of doing everything on his own terms. It so happened that Waterloo, the fashionable club adjoining the battlefield near Brussels, was looking for a British professional. Cotton applied for the job, his decision greatly influenced by the fact that Enrique Moss had been appointed Argentinian ambassador to Brussels.

Chapter 4

Cotton's seven years at Langley Park had been happy and fruitful. During that period he had emerged as the premier British golfer, had established himself as a prolific journalist, had pioneered the concept of sportsmen endorsing commercial products, had taken the first steps towards becoming a serious author by working on the manuscript of his first book of golf instruction, and had cut his teeth as a course designer by undertaking a thorough revision of Langley Park.

But his move to Waterloo emancipated him. The Belgians had no inherited preconception of what a golf professional should be or what his place should be in the social pecking order. They were interested in golf and now they had among them an absolute master of the game. Away from the club he was treated as an equal and at the club as a superior. One of the two monkeys was off his back. And now he was in a much more sympathetic atmosphere to prepare himself for the task of shrugging off the second monkey by winning the Open championship. He was exhilarated by his release from the petty snobbery of British golf, from hostile spectators who cheered when he missed a putt and from the jealousy which had tainted the Professional Golfers' Association's attitude towards him.

Professionals' shops at this time tended to be small, dark and smelling of tar and varnish, marvellous and mysterious sorcerers' dens to the boys of that era but representing everything that Cotton wanted to banish from professional golf. The shop he established at Waterloo was large, light and airy, and stocked with the latest fashions in sportswear. It would not have been out of place in Oxford Street or Fifth Avenue.

He also set up a golf school, and, of course, Toots became his most avid pupil. Contrary to his bleak prognosis on their first meeting, she proved to possess a considerable aptitude for the game. She had put her name down for lessons at Mar del Plata on the suggestion of a friend who told her that the gentle pace of the game would relax her, a gravely mistaken promise because, as events were to prove over and over again, nothing could relax the passionate nature of Toots.

Most mornings she had a lesson, diligently hitting one-handed shots to build up each arm separately, as Cotton himself did, and then playing the course with him in the afternoon. She was a short hitter by the standards of the leading women golfers and her strength, as Cotton said when she was not within earshot of an overt compliment, was in her consistency with every club in the bag. Her dedication to self-improvement, no less fervent than Cotton's, brought her down to eight handicap and she became a considerable match-player. From her experience of playing with Cotton, by now the longest straight driver in the game, she developed an immunity from the damaging complex which can afflict a player who is constantly outdriven. All that meant, so far as she was concerned, was that she and her opponent had to select different clubs for the next shot. And since she was equally at ease with all her clubs the distinction was immaterial.

Inevitably Toots moved in with Cotton. An annulment of her marriage to Enrique was out of the question because there were no grounds for one. As for divorce, it was not an option for a staunch Roman Catholic.

The union, blessed by love if not by law, transformed both their lives and revolutionised professional golf. Toots devoted all her exceptional energy to learning about the game and promoting Cotton's career. She became quite expert in rules and technical theory, although she was always prone to express golfing opinions which were eccentric to the point of poppycock. Above all she developed into a formidable businesswoman. She said of him later: "He never had a business head. If he had we'd have been multi-millionaires by now." It was a curious thing to say about a man whose legendary endorsement contracts and income from writing had made him the envy of the profession well before she took an interest in his affairs. She well understood that winning the Open was the key to their future and her extravagance, as well as her ambition for him, required that he be successful. As for that extravagance, she would have rejected the notion as nonsense. Cotton wanted the best but Toots positively demanded it.

One small incident years later, when the Cottons had been forced to auction their furniture and sell their villa and were living in an apartment in the Penina hotel, illustrates the style of Toots. A group of golf correspondents and their wives had been invited for a week of golf and relaxation by the hotel and the Cottons planned a reception for them in the apartment. Toots phoned Fortnum and Mason to send out a kilo of caviar; the drinks were in Cotton's domain. Toots was aghast at his suggestion that the visitors would be perfectly happy with Portuguese champagne. When it came to spending the hotel's money Cotton's conscience was fairly relaxed but he drew the line at ordering the prohibitively expensive French champagne from the bar. Accordingly he got word to the writers asking them if each one would pick up a couple of bottles of Moët in the duty-free shop at the airport when they left. They were more than happy to make this modest contribution to the festivities and the bottles were duly sent up to the apartment.

By the usual standards, and tastes, of the journalists, the lavish refreshments were wildly over the top. In due course Toots submitted an itemised bill for the press party to the hotel for reimbursement. The account included the champagne. The assistant manager who was presented with this work of creative accountancy knew perfectly well how the champagne had been obtained and an exchange of austere correspondence followed.

Toots was quite unabashed and argued with her usual zest that it was no business of the hotel how she had obtained the champagne and her husband must be repaid its full retail value. No journalist justifying his expenses claim could have presented the case more adroitly. The episode ranked alongside the late James Cameron's triumph after he had submitted an account for the purchase of a camel when on assignment in north Africa. An alert scrutineer at the office wrote to Cameron on his return and asked him the whereabouts of the newspaper's property, to wit, one camel. Cameron's masterly response was to include on his next claim for expenses an item: to the burial of the camel.

There was much more to Toots than a sharp operator and in some ways she was a paradoxical character. She was Cotton's severest critic and at the same time his most loyal supporter. She was a stickler for the trivia of social niceties but in no sense a snob; when young professional golfers, mostly youths from modest backgrounds, came to consult Cotton about their careers and their playing problems, she welcomed them like surrogate sons but insisted that they dress and deport themselves as if they were pupils at a finishing school. She treated Cotton in the same way. On one occasion at Penina Cotton came down to dinner wearing trousers which Toots judged to be too light for evening wear. "You must go up and change at once," she demanded. With the familiar wry smile which he used at such moments to convey the message 'Isn't she a proper caution but I might as well indulge her', he departed and returned wearing replacement trousers which he calculated to be fractionally darker. Toots was not satisfied. Cotton played the game for all it was worth, changing into another pair just a shade darker. It was not until the fifth pair of trousers that dinner was allowed to proceed, a technical victory for Toots but bought at the price of being made to look ridiculous.

At Waterloo, Cotton suffered his first defeat in skirmishes with the indomitable will of Toots. During his time at Langley Park he had taken flying lessons and he now planned to buy a light plane and fly it to tournaments in Britain. Toots detested flying and flatly vetoed the proposal. When they travelled they would do so in a civilised manner, in a luxury car or a luxury ocean liner. It has become a rigid convention in professional golf that the first thing a young player does when he wins a big cheque is to buy a flashy new car. Even in such a tiny detail as this Cotton was ahead of his time. He was a motoring fanatic all his life. He habitually bought his cars secondhand from friends, because that way he knew the history and performance of the vehicle and the price was usually favourable. He adored driving, at terrifying speed, and once drove 170 miles to an exhibition match, played 36 holes and drove home again in the evening.

Another time he drove 555 miles in eleven hours from Evreux to Bíarritz, stopping only for petrol and refills of biscuits and fruit to nibble on the road. He admitted that it was a daft thing to do but he was proud of his performance and felt he was on to a good thing when he bet £10 against the boast of three friends that they could do better. They were coming over on the night ferry to Dieppe and reckoned they would be on the road by 5 a.m. They said they would be bathed and changed and in the casino at

Biarritz before seven o'clock that night. They had over 600 miles to travel but made it easily, averaging 60 miles an hour in their 3-litre Bentley. Cotton ruefully reflected as he paid up that he had overlooked the advantage of having three drivers to share the ordeal.

Deane Beman, the commissioner of the American professional tour and a considerable player in his own right, gave it as his opinion that the major factor in improved scoring standards was the invention of power steering. Golfers of an earlier era who drove long distances to tournaments arrived with stiffened muscles and impaired sense of touch. As a youngster Cotton had believed the theory that driving was bad for golf but discovered that he was an exception and could drive for hours without being in the slightest degree affected. The secret, he claimed, was to drive a powerful car and his choice in Belgium, as a present from Toots, was a blood-red, supercharged 1929 Mercedes-Benz cabriolet to which he added 100,000 miles to the 3,000 miles of the previous owner. He claimed that it was still full of running when he sold it after thirteen years of proud ownership. The price he received for the sale, enforced because he had nowhere to keep the car at the outbreak of war, was £120 and it was a source of wistful pain to him years later as he saw his highly collectable car changing hands for five-figure sums.

It was in this magnificent beast that Cotton and Toots travelled to the 1934 Open championship at Sandwich where they had rented a house. A fuller account of that momentous week is given in Part II. At that time all competitors had to qualify for the full championship by playing two rounds on Monday and Tuesday. The first two rounds of the championship were played on Wednesday and Thursday and the last two rounds were completed on Friday.

The Cottons arrived in plenty of time for him to practise and familiarise himself with the course of the Royal St George's club. He had left nothing to chance, having practised with his usual intensity in Belgium to bring his game to championship pitch and had brought no fewer than four sets of clubs with him, a precaution which had necessitated having the spare wheels of the Mercedes fitted to the front wings so that another luggage grid could be fitted to the back.

When he went out to practise he was first perplexed, and then worried, because his game had completely deserted him. The harder he practised the worse it got. He made up his mind to withdraw from the championship but Toots was not going to give his detractors a chance to label him a quitter. In his despair Cotton decided not to touch a club at all on Sunday. A rest could certainly do him no more harm than the damage to his confidence that further practice would induce. In the event he did touch a club, as caddie for Toots. He was off early for the Monday qualifying round and played like a man inspired, eighteen of the most perfect holes he had ever played, as he described it. That took all the pressure off him and made the second qualifying round a formality. His immaculate play in the championship included a record 65, a feat celebrated by the introduction of the Dunlop 65 golf ball, and he had a nine-stroke lead as he waited to play the final round on Friday afternoon. By now the anti-hero had become the most popular of heroes and the excited crowd could not wait to hail the new champion. Indeed, to a great many of them he was the champion already, for it was unthinkable that with nine strokes in hand there could be any other result.

Cotton presented himself on the first tee at his appointed time but was told there would be a delay for a quarter of an hour while the stewards brought the crowds under control and cleared the course. In retrospect Cotton realised that he should have gone away and spent the time hitting a few shots, or putting, anything to keep his mind engaged and his muscles limber. But he was on the brink of realising his life's ambition and his one concern was to escape the back-slapping of well-wishers and other distractions of crowd hysteria. For them the championship was already won but Cotton well knew the dangers in golf of anticipating success. He went and sat by himself in a small tent by the tee. His fertile imagination explored all the ways it would be possible for him to lose the championship. He was seized with stomach cramps of such violence that he could hardly stand up. For a long time he had been on a strict diet of almost raw steak, minced carrots and mineral water, prescribed by a fashionable Parisian physician. Cotton swore that the diet had done wonders for him and that he had not deviated from it on this occasion. It must remain a matter for conjecture whether this indigestible regime was responsible for his stomach cramps, or whether his nervous excitement was to blame. At all events when he emerged from the tent he was like a ghost, in a cold sweat and a ghastly pallid colour.

His play was a feeble travesty of the golf he had produced up to then and it seemed that his nine-stroke lead might indeed not be enough to see him home. Then on the thirteenth green he holed a long putt and he relaxed. His strength returned and he finished the round with all the power and brilliance which had earned him that 65. He won by five strokes and inherited the kingdom which had obsessed him since he turned professional. In the intervening twelve years not a day had passed, when he did not think about winning the Open championship.

When he returned to Waterloo the members welcomed him back into the club through an arch of crossed golf clubs and at the celebration dinner presented him with a gold cigarette case, not the most tactful memento for a lifelong non-smoker but the gesture was appreciated. In fact, the Open championship trophy, a silver claret jug, was not the most appropriate reward for a non-drinker but a wise Belgian doctor took care of that minor detail. He prescribed a modest daily intake of red wine to supply the vital vitamins and minerals which were lacking from Cotton's faddy diets.

Cotton's triumph took care of his public image in Britain. He was now the most popular of heroes, having become the first Briton to win the Open after eleven years of overseas domination. He would never again hear cheering, or laughter, when he missed a short putt and snarl in response: "Very funny!" There remained, however, the matter of his strained relations with the Professional Golfers' Association. As the champion golfer he automatically became captain of the PGA (the post is now filled by election) and an ex-officio member of the executive committee. He attended the first meeting of the committee after the Open championship and, to the surprise of the other members, took the chair. After eleven years they were not *au fait* with this rule. Cotton took this opportunity to put his point of view about his unorthodox ways of tackling the job of being a golf professional and his ambitions for the profession. Since his championship victory had triumphantly vindicated his approach he already had the respect of his fellows and now he had their full attention. In his arrogance he had never before deigned to explain the reasoning which lay behind his individualistic ways and at least this meeting cleared the air. The maverick was welcomed into the herd. He himself wrote that he made his peace and no doubt that is how he felt at the time. It was to prove not so much a peace treaty as an uneasy truce.

All Cotton's niggling objections, or nearly all of them, to working in Britain had now been resolved. The move to Waterloo had served its purpose. As the champion golfer he could dictate his own conditions of employment. As for the indignities of having to change in the home professionals' shops when attending tournaments Cotton had long since established a routine designed to provide him with maximum comfort and subject the established conventions to maximum ridicule.

He and Toots would hire the most sumptuous limousine, a Rolls-Royce for preference, and load it with a picnic hamper from Fortnum and Mason. They would select a prominent position in the car park and use the limousine as a private mobile clubhouse, setting up a picnic table and chairs and dining *al fresco* on exotic delicacies, as if at a fashionable sporting occasion such as Twickenham or Henley. Instead of regarding this professional golfer as a visiting menial the club members, who faced the staple golf club lunch of steak and kidney pie and treacle tart, would observe the Cottons with pangs of envy. And if they suffered pangs of guilt, or even uneasy feelings of inferiority and deprivation, then that was the effect the Cottons sought to provoke. The members could hardly stop themselves from feeling absurd that their club rules forbade them offering hospitality to a man who was on familiar terms with such golfing companions as the Duke of Kent and the Prince of Wales.

So when Lord Rosebery approached Cotton with a generous offer to return home and put the Ashridge golf club on the map it did not take much persuasion before agreement was reached. After all, there would be no nonsense about excluding the champion golfer from the clubhouse. In his contract he had specified that both he and Toots would be honorary members.

Chapter 5

The first order of business arising from the move to Hertfordshire was to find a home and since Toots had such definite ideas about the kind of house which would be suitable they decided to build one close to the Ashridge club. Seldom in the history of modern domestic architecture can an architect, builder and his workmen have been so badgered and bombarded with imperious demands by a client. No detail was too small to escape her closest attention. Materials were rejected out of hand if they failed to meet her exacting specification. Slipshod workmanship had to be done again and she made it plain that they would have to go on doing it over and over again until they got it right.

The five-bedroomed house (four bathrooms), with staff quarters and a four-car garage on half an acre of land cost £5,000, at least double the normal rate for a house of this size at the time. Toots haunted the auction rooms for suitable antiques and when her dream house was finished, their first real home, they named it 'Shangri La'.

While Toots was engaged on creating the most luxurious home any professional golfer had ever before inhabited, Cotton himself was doing much the same thing with his new professional's shop, improving on the ideas he had pioneered in Belgium. There remained only the question of staff.

For those who are familiar with the caddies of this era his choice may seem eccentric. For golfers of Cotton's generation the caddie was no more than a porter. He would no more have dreamt of discussing tactics and club selection with his caddie, in the modern custom, than he would have consulted a professional coach to remedy a problem in his technique. If he had a caddie who had been attached to one club all his life and knew every nuance of the greens he would seek advice on the line of a putt, as he did with Ernest Butler when he won the championship at Royal St George's. But the itinerant caddies who worked at tournaments were mostly social misfits, drunks and vagabonds. The usual practice was to phone the caddie master and ask him to sort you out a clean one who did not smell.

Cotton used Butler whenever he could, sending him the fare to travel to tournaments. When Butler died, alone in a Sandwich boarding house, the Cottons organised and paid for his funeral, just one of many private acts of charity they performed within the golfing community. When Cotton was offered a substantial fee to take over the golf column in the *News of the World* he made it a condition of the contract that the newspaper continued to pay his predecessor, J. H. Taylor. And when the professional at Harrods was expelled from the Professional Golfers' Association, on the grounds that the Knightsbridge store was not a golf club, Cotton paid the school fees for the man's two sons.

In Belgium he had a regular caddie who used to cycle immense distances to tournaments to work for him. One day this man did not appear and it transpired that he had quarrelled with his mother over money and had been detained for murdering her with an axe.

During the 1929 Ryder Cup match Cotton played against Walter Hagen, a man who greatly influenced him not only for his dashing style both as a golfer and as a man but because the American resolutely and spectacularly refused to be treated as a second-class citizen. He was also impressed by the dapper appearance and enterprise of Hagen's young caddie. Ernest Hargreaves had been apprenticed to a tailor, hence his sense of dress, and had become interested in golf as a boy caddie at Moortown golf club in his native Leeds. He was a bright, cheeky lad and when he read that the American team was due to arrive at Southampton he travelled south, presented himself on the dockside and announced to the American captain: "I'm your caddie, sir". Hagen, assuming that the boy had been officially appointed to this duty, surrendered his golf bag. In the anarchic world of caddies there is one inviolable rule: once a caddie has shouldered a bag that act represents a binding contract. Hargreaves became Hagen's regular caddie on visits to Britain and Cotton noted with approval the young man's progress. So when Shangri La was ready Cotton engaged Hargreaves as valet, driver, handyman and caddie, an appointment considerably influenced by the fact that Hargreaves had newly married and his bride, Ivy, was an excellent cook. The domestic arrangements were completed by installing Toots' two young girls, Nelly-Maria and Isabel, or Chickie as she has been known all her life, in convent school.

This was a prosperous time for the Cottons. He had proved the theory that a man's worth is judged by his own self-evaluation and his charges were breathtaking by the standards of the day: £200 for an exhibition match, paid in advance and the cheque cleared before he played. His fee for a lesson was £10, £5 for playing a round with a pupil (it took much longer to play eighteen holes but was more enjoyable for him). He bought shares in George Nicolls, the Scottish company which manufactured the clubs he was under contract to use. Curiously, he did not stock Nicolls clubs in his shop, concentrating on selling the rival Scottish brand of Ben Sayers and also Wilson clubs which he imported directly from America.

His private generosity did not extend to the business. On one occasion Hargreaves was in Cotton's study in Shangri La with him when the assistant, Bruce Thorpe, came in and announced that he had just sold a customer a full set of clubs and a new golf bag. He added that in view of the size of this sale he had thrown in three golf balls. Cotton was furious and sent Thorpe running after the customer to exact payment for the balls.

Anyone born since the egalitarian revolution of post-war Britain may find it difficult to appreciate the achievement and impact which Cotton made by his lonely fight to emancipate his profession. In 1938 the 'cats', or working classes, who made up the mass of the population, might *look* at a king, but in a duly deferential manner. This cat had made himself a king, as Willie Whitelaw was astonished to discover. The future Viscount Whitelaw, power behind Margaret Thatcher's throne and keeper of the Conservative party conscience, was then a member of the Cambridge University golf team which went to Ashridge for a week's coaching.

Like all amateur golfers of the day, he had been brought up to regard the professional as a club servant, on a level with the steward, a man to be respected for his skills but employed, above all, to do the members' bidding. It came as a considerable culture shock therefore to meet the forbidding figure of Cotton. He utterly dominated the undergraduates right from the start with his cool, calculated and abrasive manner. They were in awe of this man who had pulled such a comprehensive role reversal on them. He commanded and they jumped. They had been taught the received wisdom of golf, that it was a game of all left arm, and Cotton quickly disabused them. He made them work immensely hard, bringing to his coaching the same intensity of dedication that had transformed his own game.

At the end of the first day's labours Cotton's mood changed completely. The austere disciplinarian became a gracious host, hospitable, friendly and very good fun. This ability to change persona was to bewilder many of his friends. When they went to watch him play they would naturally enough call out a greeting and the stone-faced Cotton would cut them dead, not even acknowledging the greeting with a glance of recognition. For his part, he considered such social intrusions into his professional life nothing less than an impertinence. He used to say: "You wouldn't dream of barging into the offices of a large company during a board meeting and shout 'Good luck, Charles' at the chairman just because you happened to know him socially. The golf course is my office and I need to concentrate fully on my business." Once he had handed in his card he reverted to his usual gregarious nature and was delighted to see the friends he had just studiously ignored.

Whitelaw and his companions fell under the Cotton spell, recognising him to be an exceptional teacher as well as a wonderful player. During the Open championship at Carnoustie that year Whitelaw went to watch Cotton. He was familiar with Cotton's majestic striking by now but he marvelled at the courage Cotton displayed in battling against the elements. His verdict, looking back over Cotton's career, was that he did much more than change the whole profession; he also had a great influence on amateur golf.

Like his father, Cotton had an inventive mind and kept coming up with ideas. He was years ahead of the market when he designed an electric cart for golfers. He had it built by Kingston Motors and it was powered by two twelve-volt batteries. It worked well enough but its narrow wheel base made it unstable on steep slopes and for safety reasons Cotton had to reserve it for his own use. Another scheme which came to nothing arose from his conviction that the sound of club-face making impact with the ball was an important factor in helping a golfer play well. He wrote to his clubmakers and asked if they could design a slotted shaft which would reproduce the sound made by the club striking the old gutta-percha golf balls. When he blistered his thumb through excessive practice he wore one of Toots' kid gloves and soon a Henry Cotton golf glove was on sale, adding to the stream of royalties from his book and Cotton golf shoes (2d a pair royalty on the most popular brand of shoes from a contract which ran for twenty-five years).

As a journalist he was more prolific, and much better paid, than professional golf correspondents. All the hard work of his youth was paying off even more handsomely than he had ever dreamed. And then he greatly increased his earning capacity by winning the Open for the second time, at Carnoustie in 1937.

On the way home the Cottons stopped near Reading to compete in the Calcot mixed foursomes. This was to be Toots' day, as she made quite clear. Henry had enjoyed his hour of glory; now it was her turn. She gave him his orders: "Don't you dare put me in the rough. You know I don't like playing out of the rough and I do not want to let my public down." Straight as he was, probably the straightest long driver in modern golf, Cotton was not super-human and inevitably one of his drives strayed into the light rough. Toots had gone on ahead in approved foursomes procedure so as to be ready to play her shot without undue delay. To the bewilderment of 'her' public, she pulled out her spoon and hit the ball with all the power of her raging fury straight back towards the tee. Cotton loved telling this story at dinner parties because someone was sure to ask: "What on earth did you do next?" What he did was to make a typical riposte to his wife's reversion to the old Flemish game of chole, in which a team of two players hit the ball towards a target while the opponent, the decholeur, sought to thwart their progress by playing every third shot, hitting the ball into the worst trouble he could find. Without betraying by word or gesture that anything untoward had occurred, Cotton walked up to the ball, took out his brassie and hit a stupendous shot to within two feet of the flagstick. Toots holed the putt, remarking robustly: "That's the only way to treat you, Cotton. You haven't been trying up to now." They won the tournament but Cotton always treasured that competition as a rare and notable victory in their enduring battle of the sexes.

He also competed in the Ryder Cup match at Southport and Ainsdale which proved to be memorable not for the result, another overwhelming victory for the United States, but for the quick-witted grace of the American captain in his acceptance speech. Walter Hagen had made some notes and stuffed them in the pocket of his overcoat. He then took off the coat and laid it on a chair, so when he was called to the podium he searched his jacket pockets in vain and then had to ad lib. Blandly he announced: "I am honoured to captain the first United States team to win on home soil." The crowd stirred visibly and audibly at this gaffe and Hagen pretended to look nonplussed. Then he raised four fingers, indicating the four Open championships he had won in Britain, and added: "You can't blame me for feeling at home over here." The crowd cheered him for a full five minutes.

Following his second Open championship triumph an attractive offer was made to Cotton to tour Europe for a series of exhibition matches and to play in the continental Open championships. As always the Cottons did it in style, by chauffeured limousine. Cotton was invincible on this trip and while winning the German Open at Bad Ems he met an English amateur golfer who was to become a lifelong friend. John de Forest was a considerable golfer who had won the Amateur Championship and represented Great Britain in the Walker Cup match of 1932. He was to achieve international fame after the war when playing in the United States Masters tournament for an incident in which his approach shot lodged in the bank of the creek in front of the thirteenth green. The ball lay up to its waist in water and de Forest decided to play it, rather than drop the ball back onto the fairway under penalty. He removed the shoe and sock from his right foot, rolled up his trouser leg and then planted his bare right foot firmly on the bank and stepped into the water with his fully shod left foot. His look of incredulity as he realised what he had done added hugely to the amusement of the spectators. The laughter turned to enthusiastic applause as he played a wonderful recovery shot and holed his ten-foot putt for a birdie.

At the time of his meeting with the Cottons, de Forest was second secretary at the Paris embassy under Sir Alfred Duff Cooper and marked down for a distinguished career in the diplomatic service which, indeed, he went on to achieve. His public persona as a staid diplomat was somewhat at odds, however, with his roistering life off duty. Only two things marred the perfection of life for John de Forest: the fact that his father kept him on a tight financial rein and that candles were limited to two ends for burning simultaneously. This parental discipline was understandable since Count de Bendern had paid off King Edward VII's gambling debts and detected in his own son an equal talent for profligacy. As a young undergraduate de Forest had shown himself to be a prime candidate for P. G. Wodehouse's Drones club and had been forced to supplement his allowance by taking a job as a van driver. Many a debutante had been driven home from dances in the delivery van, with de Forest going straight on to work still in his white tie and tails.

On this tour of Europe Cotton, although de Forest's junior by a year, was charged with the duty of sending newspaper cuttings to Count de Bendern as proof that his son really was playing golf rather than playing the giddy goat. Actually, de Forest did both with equal dedication, winning the Amateur championships of Czechoslovakia and Austria by day and painting the town red by night. Cotton was mystified throughout the tour by the listless appearance of his chauffeur, an exceptionally handsome young man called Charlie. He then discovered that de Forest and a few of the other British amateurs had been keeping Charlie up all hours, taking him out on the town to attract girls to their parties.

Cotton was engaged to play an exhibition match in Vienna and Toots took the opportunity to play in the Austrian Women's Amateur championship. The competition proved to be a double triumph because it gave Cotton a chance to gain his revenge on Toots. Just before the French Open Cotton had been putting badly because, as she felt, he was using a putter which was not suitable. He was furious when he discovered on the first hole of the championship that his putter was missing from his golf bag and that a putter belonging to Toots had been substituted. He scanned the gallery but she was nowhere to be seen, a most unusual circumstance in itself since, except for one week when she was indisposed, she walked every step of the way with him for every championship round he ever played. In fact she was present on this occasion but keeping out of sight. Just to spite her he considered putting with an iron but his sense of golfing propriety prevailed and he took out her putter. Somewhat to his annoyance he holed putt after putt and only then did Toots reveal herself, her expression a picture of vindication.

In the women's championship Toots played her way steadily through the preliminary rounds to the final when her opponent was the powerful Maryla Gross, seeking her third success in the championship. It was a long course and it seemed that the strength of her opponent must prevail when Toots went five down with twelve holes to play. This was Cotton's chance. He castigated her with the phrases she had hurled at him over the years. She was gutless. She simply had not been trying. There was nothing worse in golf than a quitter. She must show a bit of character and buckle down to the job in hand. Toots channelled her fury into her golf and went on to win the championship, the pinnacle of her golfing career. The two amateur champions, Toots and John de Forest, were photographed together holding their trophies. Cotton was inordinately proud of what he claimed was 'his' victory.

He never put much store by his own almost routine victories in the European Open championships because they did not attract many of the leading British professionals and so he was not tested by worthy opposition. But there was one occasion when he was extremely hard pressed to assert his supremacy, in the 1938 Italian Open championship at Sestriere.

On the evening of the first day of the championship the American professional, Joe Ezar, entertained the crowd with his exhibition of trick shots. The president of the club was so impressed by this display of wizardry that when he paid Ezar his fee he remarked that with such skills at his command it was a wonder that the course record was still intact. The conversation was continued in Ezar's natural habitat, the bar. The course record, which Cotton had tied in each of the first two rounds, was 67 and Ezar enquired how much the president would offer for a 66. The president thought that a 66 might be worth a thousand lire. And a 65? Two thousand lire. Would the president double the kitty again to four thousand lire for a 64? Certainly. And what if Ezar nominated his score on each of the 18 holes to make up that 64? The president offered a suitable bonus if Ezar could perform such a miracle. Ezar borrowed the president's packet of cigarettes and wrote down the scores hole by hole by which he proposed to score 64. The deal was struck. Ezar caught the barman's eye and went into serious training.

The next morning the comatose Ezar had to be shaken from his drunken stupor and carried into a cold shower before displaying the first signs of life. His prospects of going out and performing an unprecedented feat of golfing virtuosity seemed to be nil, and hardly brighter when he stumbled onto the first tee in a feverish sweat, shivering and draped in his voluminous camel-hair coat even though the weather was calm and warm. He slipped off the coat, handed it to the caddie, took his driver and hit a beauty right up the middle of the fairway. For nine holes, wearing his camel-hair coat as he walked between shots, he scored exactly as he had nominated, to be out in 32. On the second half he blew his bonus by taking four strokes at a short hole he had nominated for a three. But at the next hole, a difficult par-four where he had nominated four, he made three. Apart from that transposition, Ezar stuck to the scenario he had outlined on the cigarette packet and came home in 32 to win his four thousand lire. Cotton won with rounds of 67, 67, 68, 66 and Ezar finished in second place.

With his pockets full of money Ezar embarked on an epic spending spree and was flat broke when the golf season ended. The sportswriter Trevor Wignall was booked on the *Queen Mary* to America and was surprised on entering his cabin to find Ezar's grinning face peeping from the wardrobe. Wignall could not harbour a stowaway for the entire passage and insisted that Ezar throw himself on the mercy of the purser. He did so and, not for the first time, had to work his passage home, giving golf lessons and exhibitions for the passengers.

The Cottons returned home to the depressing atmosphere of approaching catastrophe. Adolf Hitler was flexing his ego and the talk was all about Munich and the possibility of having to go to war. The Cottons dined in London with friends and one of the other guests, the American impresario Charles Tucker who lived and worked in London, insisted that there would be no war. He backed his conviction by promising that when Neville Chamberlain made an accommodation with Hitler he would give the same party a slap-up dinner and put Cotton on the music halls. After Chamberlain returned with his "Peace in our time" announcement, Tucker was as good as his word and invited the Cottons to a celebratory dinner. "What about the music hall?" asked Cotton. Tucker replied that he was opening at the Coliseum on December 5th. Cotton was to have fifteen minutes as top of the bill.

He worked up an act involving instruction and entertainment, hitting balls into a net and soft balls into the audience. The most difficult part, he found, was to discipline himself to repeat exactly the same movements and the same words he had written in his script so as to provide cues for the electricians to time the lighting changes. Under the guidance of the theatre manager, Sam Harbour, Cotton polished his act, with Hargreaves acting as caddie and handing him the clubs. In one section he used shoes, club, gloves and balls treated with phosphorescent paint under blue light on a darkened stage.

Brigadier-General A. C. Critchley, a noted amateur golfer and spiritual leader of the amateurs who regularly toured on the continent and called themselves 'Critchley's Circus', booked the first two rows of the stalls for his golfing friends to give Cotton a mass raspberry. But even they were so impressed by Cotton's act that they gave him a two-minute ovation. Cotton went through his routine twice nightly, and three times on Saturday, and for weeks afterwards businessmen were observed at St Martin's Lane demonstrating how Cotton did it as they walked to work. Cotton was held over for a second week and was such a success that he was offered £10,000 by the Empire Circuit for a sixteen-week tour of the provincial variety halls.

The approach of war killed that deal but Cotton was still confident enough of the future to play in and win the 1939 German Open championship at Bad Ems. John de Forest also competed in that championship and afterwards they both went off for a celebratory party given by Carl Henkel, president of the German Golf Federation. (Henkel was killed in the war but in 1945 his secretary sent Cotton a cheque for his 1939 prize winnings.) The restaurant was packed with young Germans in a high state of excitement at the approaching prospect of hostilities. Every few moments someone would jump up with raised glass and shout: "Heil Hitler!" to a tumultuous response. Every time this happened John de Forest followed suit, leaping up and shouting at the top of his voice: "Fuck you!" The language may not have been in the highest traditions of the British diplomatic service but it most certainly expressed the feelings of the nation.

Mr and Mrs George Cotton.

Posing for a picture.

With his first trophy, aged sixteen, in 1923.

With his brother Leslie.

Opposite At Foxgrove, aged twenty.

Right Leaving for the United States, 1928.

Below The revised swing in more upright plane.

Putting. You can see from his stance why he had to be carried off the green after a long session.

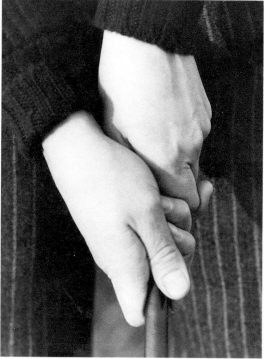

The grip.

Opposite Off the first tee at the 1930 *News of the World* finals, with Charles Whitcombe.

The Austin Sheerline, 1949.

With Titch who died soon after of a broken heart.

The donkey Pacifico.

Exercising on the Gym Bar.

Marriage to Toots in 1939.

'Shangri La'.

Above left A putting machine.

Above The automatic tee-er.

Mobile golf ball driving
machine.

RAF dinghies at Monte Carlo.

Chapter 6

*T*he certainty of impending war presented the Cottons with a crisis of conscience. As an Argentinian citizen Toots would have to register as an alien and was liable to be interned on the Isle of Man for the duration of the hostilities. Every possible solution to this dilemma seemed unthinkable. Skipping off together to a safe haven was out of the question, although that option was seized by some and they were reviled as bomb dodgers as they settled comfortably in places such as Bermuda. Separation, with Toots taking up residence in, say, Switzerland, was equally intolerable. Until now Toots had not considered divorce as a possibility because there was no mechanism within the Roman Catholic church by which her marriage to Enrique Moss could be dissolved. It was a contract for life. The threat of internment was a civil matter, however, and she reasoned that in the exceptional circumstances a civil solution would not greatly change her irregular status in the eyes of the church. After all, the church would not recognise her divorce but it was not the ecclesiastical authorities who were about to intern her.

On June 20, 1939, the district court of Liepaja, Latvia, determined "to divorce by the husband's default the matrimony contract on September 12, 1921, between Enrique Moss and Isabel Moss, born Estanguet; to leave in their mother's education the daughter Nelly-Maria Moss, born of this matrimony in Argentina on September 9, 1922, and the daughter Isabel-Maria Moss, born on May 17, 1928".

Cotton had served in the Officers' Training Corps at Alleyn's and, with his flying experience, he was automatically commissioned in the Administrative and Special Duties Branch of the Royal Air Force Voluntary Reserve as a probationary pilot officer in July and ordered to report for an initial training course at the officers' school, RAF Loughborough, in August. The notification from the Air Ministry added: "Please bring your civilian pattern respirator with you."

He was next posted to RAF Shawbury, near Shrewsbury, and appointed catering officer in addition to his other administrative duties. His obsession with diets could now be exercised on a grand scale. Observing the popularity of bread and butter pudding, he experimented with the ingredients, his specification calling for a higher and higher raisin and sultana content, much to the approval of the airmen. He became, as he recalled, a thorough bread and butter pudding bore until one day he received a parcel containing a slab of bread and butter pudding nailed to a board.

He moved on to RAF Halton which, by one of those coincidences which sometimes favoured servicemen with good connections in high places, happened to be five miles from Ashridge. The posting was a consolation for his disappointment at being turned down for flying training on account of his age since he had hoped that his civilian flying licence would qualify him for selection to become a Spitfire pilot.

The Latvian divorce had not satisfied the authorities and Cotton's wedding licence expired before Toots was able to obtain an Argentinian divorce.

Finally the way was clear and that December he and Toots were married at Westminster register office in the presence of four witnesses, Lord Rosebery, Lord Castlerosse, John Burroughs and P. B. (Laddie) Lucas, the finest left-hand golfer, amateur or professional, Britain had produced, and soon to become a fighter pilot ace flying Hurricanes.

Valentine Castlerosse was a particular favourite of Cotton's, a keen if erratic golfer because one of his elbows had been demolished during the first world war. He created the celebrated Killarney golf course on his family estate in County Kerry and because of his wide circle of society friends he was employed by Lord Beaverbrook as a gossip columnist on the *Sunday Express*. He was a noted wit. At a reception a woman surveyed his bulky frame and remarked: "Why Lord Castlerosse, if that stomach was on a woman I'd say she was pregnant." He replied: "Madame, twenty minutes ago it was, and she isn't."

After the civil ceremony the newlyweds went to Berkhamsted to seek a blessing on their union and the priest refused to allow the Cottons to enter the church.

Toots took a job serving in the officers' mess at Halton and Cotton's duties as adjutant to a training wing were not exactly arduous. They were able to spend plenty of time together at Shangri La and a more relaxed war could not be imagined. That was one of the problems. Cotton felt that he was not making his due contribution and, of course, suffered extreme frustration over the loss of his prime years as a golfer. That frustration was increased rather than dissipated when he was able to put his golfing talents into the war effort by playing exhibition matches around the country to raise funds for the Red Cross. These proved to be highly popular and raised more than £70,000, the equivalent of a squadron of Spitfires, for the charity and an MBE for him.

A chance meeting profoundly changed Cotton's life. Church parades were held on Sundays and Roman Catholics were ordered to fall out and be marched off to the local Catholic church. One Sunday it fell to Cotton to take charge of this detail and he paraded his men with full pomp and ceremony, left, right, left, right, swing those arms, heads up, chests out, bags of swank, squad halt, left turn and so on. The young priest who was standing by the church gate asked Cotton if it was really necessary to subject the men to such rigorous military discipline whilst they were on their way to an act of religious devotion. Cotton was taken aback. He had not inherited his father's non-conformist zeal and had never been troubled by questions about the spiritual content of life. He appreciated that Toots' faith was the paramount element in her existence but for himself golf was the god which consumed all his physical, mental and spiritual energies. From that unpromising introduction the two men struck up a friendship and over the ensuing weeks the Jesuit priest, Father Peter Blake, gave Cotton instruction and converted him to the Roman Catholic faith. From then on he exemplified the truism that there are 'none so devout as converts'. Father Peter remained a friend for life. His first act of kindness was to arrange for advertisements for Cotton's exhibition matches to be displayed free of charge in the *Catholic Times*.

Cotton's conversion did nothing to dispel his feelings about the purposeless nature of his current existence. His fits of depression became deeper and more frequent, aggravated by the fact that an arsonist had torched the thatch-roofed clubhouse at Ashridge, completely destroying it along with his shop and most of its stock. Cotton was at home at the time, ordered to bed for six weeks on a diet of milk and junket which he loathed, on account of his stomach ulcer. His prescribed routine was complete rest, with no telephone, just reading, writing and sleeping. The first he knew of the fire was when he was awakened at midnight by the local police sergeant checking that he was not the culprit who had stuffed a paraffin-soaked rag into the clubhouse thatch. Toots and some friends had managed to save a considerable number of small items from the shop, Cotton's clubs, his precious hoard of golf balls and a few pieces of furniture. These they carried onto the nearby putting green out of harm's way and, with the fire now out, they retired for what remained of the night. After breakfast Toots went out to retrieve the salvaged items and discovered that everything had been stolen.

Despite the insurance, the episode represented a considerable disaster and further depressed Cotton whose morale at being laid up in bed was at a low ebb anyway. His civilian life had gone up in smoke and his service aspirations to become a fighter pilot had evaporated.

He was, as he felt, no more than a stooge and wrote in self-pitying terms to his old friend Raymond Oppenheimer. The reply was slightly surprising, even from the world's pre-eminent authority on bull-terriers.

I am sorry you feel as you do. I have had some of it myself and examined my feelings with my extremely analytical brain and came to the conclusion which has helped me and I think will help you. I do not think that you and I are upset by being stooges but in a stooge job we cannot for obvious reasons be madly interested. Now in these days it is difficult to have an outside interest because there is so little doing and if you do play golf well there is little satisfaction because you know you can do that anyway and there is no looking forward, saying "Good, feel confident now for the *News of the World* [tournament]" because there isn't one. Now you see where I am heading. The present circumstances have killed our interest in life because we have no specific event to which to look forward with zest and that is hopeless for people of our temperament who are restless, quick witted and have never sat still and done nothing.

Now I have a suggestion to you. You must force or create a small outside interest for yourself to which you can turn at once during days of boredom and depression and the obvious one that occurs to me is bull-terriers. You realise that I am only suggesting a temporary expedient and not one to last you into peace, although I may say a study of breeding and pedigrees is one of sufficiently engrossing interest to absorb the quickest intellect.

There was no question of sticking to fancy diets in the RAF and Cotton blamed this deprivation for a serious worsening of his stomach disorders. The medical officers were more prosaic, diagnosing a duodenal ulcer. Cotton had an operation and was given a medical discharge from the service. Now he felt even more of a stooge, being unable even to continue his fund-raising exhibitions for the Red Cross. There was nothing else for it but to try the bull-terrier therapy. In fact Oppenheimer's suggestion was not as eccentric as it might appear. Cotton was enormously sentimental about animals and grew increasingly so in later years. In Belgium he had a dachshund called Titch which had to go into quarantine when the Cottons moved back to Britain. The six-month separation broke the dog's heart, by Cotton's diagnosis, and he died soon after being released. A farmer donated a lamb for auction at one of the Red Cross exhibitions but nobody made a bid so Cotton took it home as a family pet, joining Bunny the rabbit. The problem was that everywhere the Cottons went the lamb was sure to go, and after invading their bedroom a few times it really did have to go. The friendship and unquestioning loyalty of his pets was to become an increasing source of solace and it is probably true to say that towards the end of his life he esteemed his dogs as highly as his friends.

At this period he doted on Johnny, a bull-terrier which Oppenheimer had given him, and for a while Cotton did indeed study the books which Oppenheimer sent him. He took some comfort from looking up Johnny's pedigree and discovering that his dog was of undoubtedly aristocratic stock. In Cotton's personal order of precedence royalty and the aristocracy ranked only slightly behind the highest estate to which mankind is heir, the millionaire. Johnny had a habit of dashing out of the Cottons' gate into the road and was hit by a passing car. A broken hip and many weeks in a plaster cast did not break him of this habit, although a permanent limp slowed him down slightly. He acquired a police record after two unprovoked attacks on passers-by but charges were never pressed.

Chapter 7

*A*fter the war the Cottons sold Shangri La and settled into the penthouse suite at the Dorchester and tried to pick up the threads of their pre-war life. His first concern was to get tournament golf restarted and through his connections with the Carr family, the owners of the *News of the World*, he persuaded the newspaper to sponsor its own tournament for a prize fund of £2,000. It was a logical development because Cotton's weekly golf column had given the *News of the World* a reputation as the premier newspaper for golf, certainly in the popular press.

When he attended the next meeting of the PGA committee in the association's tiny headquarters office in Bishopsgate the honorary secretary, Commander R. C. T. Roe RN (Rtd), rattled through the minutes of the previous meeting. Roe was a former submariner, an extremely able administrator but a man of autocratic temperament. His committee style was in the best naval tradition, that is the salty tradition as exemplified in the Hornblower novels rather than Winston Churchill's stark dictum about the tradition of the Royal Navy being 'nothing but rum, sodomy and the lash'.

Having addressed the ship's company from the quarterdeck, Commander Roe added, almost as an afterthought: "Oh, we've had an offer to promote a new tournament by the *News of the World* but I've turned it down because the prize money was too high. It would unbalance the tournament programme and unsettle our other sponsors." Cotton was aghast and assumed the role of Fletcher Christian. He rallied his brother professionals to his cause, pointing out that he had devoted his career to improving the lot of the profession. They must go forward. Faced with a mutiny led by a brother officer and a gentleman, Commander Roe realised that he could not intimidate Cotton and grudgingly gave way. The *News of the World* tournament was approved and became a great success.

Cotton was anxious to resume his own career, but following the major abdominal operation to deal with his ulcer and two serious illnesses, he was in no condition for the rigours of tournament golf and he therefore welcomed an invitation to help restore the Monte Carlo golf club to playing condition. The change, he hoped, would be as good as a rest. Besides, Toots was also unwell and wanted to consult a French doctor, on the grounds that they were the only ones who understood women. In the event her problem proved to be relatively trivial and easily treated but the doctor told Cotton: "You are the one who is unwell."

After treatment for a liver complaint Cotton began to feel stronger and he took a charcoal-burning Hotchkiss taxi to the top of Mont Agel to inspect what remained of the golf course. He found a French corporal and some forty German prisoners of war who were confined in the fort on the summit as they awaited repatriation. Goats and sheep had dislodged stones from the mountain paths as they descended to graze the fairways and greens and the first task was to remove these stones which covered the course. The French military commander gave permission for the prisoners to work on the course under Cotton's direction and they enjoyed this break from their boredom. As the course was gradually reinstated into playing condition and the first tourist began to arrive, the Société des Bains de Mer, which owned the property as well as the casino, invited Cotton to accept a consultancy. This started an association which was to last for eight years and provide the Cottons with the opportunity to spend their winters on the Riviera, much to the delight of Toots who greatly enjoyed a modest flutter in the casino.

Cotton had been pondering the idea of a golf school in Monte Carlo, the difficulty being that there could be no question of building a conventional driving range in a city where every expensive square foot of land was in demand for building development. It struck him that the only solution would be to hit golf balls out to sea, and the perfect location for such a project would be the lawns below the casino parapet. This area was used for *Tir aux Pigeons*, the French sporting pastime of shooting pigeons whose wings have been clipped. The effect of clipping the wings before the pigeons are released from their traps is to produce an eccentric flight pattern which adds zest to the pleasure of blasting the mutilated birds to smithereens. Presumably it also brings a comforting reassurance to the sportsmen that the birds are rendered incapable of circling and attacking the brave marksmen.

Cotton's plan was to convert this area into putting greens and an elevated tee from which floating golf balls could be hit into the sea. Nets suspended from war surplus RAF inflatable dinghies would contain the balls within the designated driving area and could be retrieved by rowing boat. The Société des Bains de Mer enthusiastically approved Cotton's proposal and the project became a big success. When the sea was too rough for the boatmen to go out and retrieve the balls, play was confined to practice nets set up in the former pigeon roosts.

Curiously, for neither was he fully fit nor his game in championship trim, Cotton played the best 72 holes of his life in 1946 when he won the French Open championship by fifteen strokes from the Belgian star, Flory van Donck, at St Cloud. He had rounds of 70, 66, 67, and 66. His total of 269 was 31 strokes under the course's scratch rating, or 19 under par in modern terms. He commented: "I am really on holiday and I felt in the best mood from the start of this championship." That same year he won the 'Star' tournament over 100 holes at Wentworth with a total of 375, adding a record 65 for the east course to set alongside his record 64 for the west course.

That year the American team won the Walker Cup, the amateur equivalent of the professionals' Ryder Cup, at St Andrews. Cotton reported the match for his newspaper and afterwards, following his usual gracious habit of sending notes to everyone who had helped him in any way or who had performed a notable achievement in golf, he sent his congratulations to the American captain, Francis Ouimet. The hero of that historic victory over the English champions, Vardon and Ray, in winning the 1913 US Open championship, was by now a respected elder statesman of the game and soon to become the first American captain of the Royal and Ancient golf club of St Andrews. Ouimet's reply stands as a definition of what international sport should be:

Dear Henry. It is difficult for me to tell you how much I appreciate your sincere note of congratulation over the success of our Walker Cup team at St Andrews. You have clearly demonstrated to me that you are not only a great golfer but a good sportsman as well. In the heat of competition this quality is sometimes forgotten or overlooked but I will carry back to my country happy thoughts of your genuine friendship. Such acts do our people and your people more good than the winning of any cup. I only hope that when the tide turns – as it surely must someday – we will not be lacking in extending to you and your friends our heartfelt felicitations, although I doubt our ability to do so as adequately as you have. May every shot you hit on the golf course and in the game of life go true to the mark always. My warmest regards to you and Toots. If I can ever be useful to you both on my side of the Atlantic do not hesitate to call upon me anytime for anything. Thanks and good luck. Sincerely, Francis Ouimet.

There was considerable doubt whether it would be possible to revive the Ryder Cup match in 1947. The British players were out of form after six years of war service and the PGA's coffers were empty. Robert Hudson, a Canadian industrialist and golf philanthropist, came to the rescue and the British Isles team sailed for America with Cotton as playing captain. As an exercise in promoting international goodwill the match, at Portland, Oregon, was not a success. Ill feeling was prompted by Cotton's formal complaint that some of the American players had roughened the faces of their iron clubs to impart extra backspin on the ball. This was no less than the truth; the American clubs were illegal, recognised as such and replaced. The trouble was that Cotton's remarks were enhanced by journalistic zeal and thoroughly outraged the American players who took their revenge by trouncing the visitors by 11 points to 1. Nevertheless, this was a serious issue that Cotton had raised because American professional golf had undoubtedly fallen into some bad habits. Commercial interests were dominating the game. Rules governing the permitted number of clubs, the form of clubs and certain procedures had been tacitly allowed to go by the board and the professionals were playing a different game from the rest of the golfing community.

Cotton was pressed to return to the United States the following spring to compete in the Masters tournament. The organisers insisted that his presence would render a service to golf and he would also be able to see that a major tournament could be run strictly in accordance with the Rules of Golf. Cotton was happy to accept the invitation. The trip would enable him to build up his strength with plenty of steaks and fresh fruit in preparation for the 1948 Open championship. He won a major tournament at White Sulphur Springs, West Virginia, before moving on to Augusta, Georgia.

A dinner party was arranged, ostensibly to celebrate the presence of the president of the United States Golf Association, Fielding Wallace, and the president of the Professional Golfers' Association, Ed Dudley. It proved to be a summit meeting of golf. Bobby Jones, whose name was synonymous with honesty and sportsmanship, took the chair and Cotton's views on the gulf between the professionals and the governing bodies were solicited. The mood was amicable and constructive, even more so after Ed Dudley announced: "The PGA will support the USGA one hundred per cent in all rules of golf. There should be only one set of rules." That informal meeting was to have a profound influence on golf for from then on the American professionals took pride in their meticulous observance of the Rules of Golf and set a public example of honesty and sportsmanship which endures to this day.

Cotton's first club appointment after being medically discharged from the RAF was with Coombe Hill at Kingston-on-Thames but it was not long before he resigned to take up an appointment at another London club, Royal Mid Surrey where he remained for six years. This club therefore enjoyed the distinction of having its professional win the Open championship, Cotton's third, at Muirfield in 1948. The victory crowned his career and confirmed his status as one of the two finest golfers, with Harry Vardon, that England had ever produced. Like Vardon, Cotton had been the best in the world. It would be invidious to try to assess which of the two was the greater player. They were from different eras and played under different conditions with different equipment. Both made profound contributions to the game of golf, Vardon as an innovator of a technique which raised the standard of golf to a higher plateau and as a potent populariser of the game in the new world, and Cotton who led the professionals into a land flowing with respect and rewards. Cotton must also receive much of the credit for turning golf into a popular spectator sport.

One of Cotton's closest friends was Henry Longhurst, the golf correspondent of the *Sunday Times* and a considerable amateur golfer in his own right. He was responsible for coining Cotton's *nom de guerre* of Maestro and he had seen all the leading players of the day so his assessment of Cotton's golf is probably as valid as anyone's: "It is impossible to imagine anyone hitting the ball better than Cotton at his best." Longhurst was in America at the time of the 1948 Open and he wrote a letter of congratulation, reading in part: "Marvellous, stupendous, colossal, surprising and immensely gratifying! I never thought you would win it again, with all the other things in your life than tearing your guts out at golf, but nobody in the world could have been more pleased. It's like old times again! Something out of the solid and much to be regretted past – regretted, I mean, in that it has gone, in most aspects of life completely."

Although the Muirfield Open was Cotton's greatest triumph in 1948 it was by no means his only distinction. That victory in the White Sulphur Springs Invitational tournament at The Greenbrier in West Virginia had given him extra satisfaction because he felt he had never received his due recognition in America. The Americans felt, and with some justification, that a golfer could not be regarded as one of the greats of the game until he had proved his worth on the game's toughest proving ground, the US Tour. Cotton never gave himself a real opportunity to make a lasting impact on American golf by campaigning there for any prolonged length of time. He had great respect and admiration for the leading American players, particularly for their professionalism and dedicated hard work, both virtues which he had emulated ever since his first visit as a teenager. But the gypsy life of driving huge distances between events, living in commercial hotels and playing tournaments week after week held no appeal for him. He was not tempted to give up his luxurious life in Britain and Europe for the sake of a bubble reputation in America. If he had anything to prove, he would prove it at the Open championship which was attended by all the great players, especially in those years when the American Ryder Cup team was visiting Britain, and was effectively the championship of the world.

Another triumph of 1948 was the publication of his book, *This Game of Golf*, which established him as a best-selling author. The initial print run of 20,000 copies was sold out immediately. Its mixture of instruction and reminiscence found a market well beyond the hard-core golfing readership, and by the end of the decade it had gone to six editions.

Cotton's health broke down again in 1949. He decided not to defend his Open championship title and he had to inform the PGA that he would not be available to play in the Ryder Cup match to be held at Ganton. Once again the match was a public relations disaster. The American captain, Ben Hogan, insisted on a tit-for-tat examination of the British team's clubs and Dick Burton had to work through the night filing down the grooves of his irons. The Americans were given thoroughly unsatisfactory accommodation and could not wait to get home once the match, which they won, was over. They cancelled their plans to play in the *Daily Telegraph* tournament. Cotton, home from a holiday in Argentina with Toots, was invited to compete in this tournament to give the event some star quality. Once again he found himself at odds with his brother professionals, many of whom threatened to 'strike'. Their reasons for announcing that they would withdraw from the tournament was that Cotton had not qualified. His name was not in the year's averages because he had played only one tournament that year. The rebels were firmly told by the sponsor that the tournament would go ahead without them but it might very well not be promoted at all the following year. The rebellion collapsed. Alan Hoby wrote in the *Sunday Express*: "What seems so despicable to me is that most of this underground vendetta can be traced to one thing – jealousy. There is a feeling among certain of his rivals that he gets too much publicity. Of course he does! For Cotton is a giant. His colourful personality would need a bucket to hold it. The others need a thimble."

In 1951 Cotton received a letter from Temple golf club, near Maidenhead, reading as follows:

My committee asked me to write to you and say that, at their last meeting, it was a unanimous wish that you should be invited to be an Honorary Member of Temple, in recognition of your great service to the game of golf in general and to British professional golf in particular. My committee further wish me to add that they hope, if you accept this invitation, you will not regard it as an empty honour, but on the contrary, that you will make frequent use of the club, where you can be assured of a warm welcome from your fellow members. Yours sincerely, T. B. C. Piggot, Secretary.

* * *

Professional golf had at last become emancipated and invited in out of the cold, helped by Cotton's campaigning over the previous quarter of a century.

The following year Cotton left Royal Mid Surrey and joined Temple as the club's professional, at the invitation of his good friend, Raymond Oppenheimer. Oppenheimer had a sumptuous apartment built for the Cottons at Temple and when the Cottons left at the end of his contract Toots asked the club to buy the expensive fittings she had added to the apartment. When the club declined she took a golf club and went on a rampage of destruction, smashing some £3,000 worth of light fittings and furnishings. Cotton also indulged in violent exercise but of a more conventional nature.

When Cotton retired from serious competitive golf his game deteriorated and consequently his enthusiasm for playing suffered. In addition to his disappointment at playing so poorly in the few events he did enter, and in his social golf, he found that the absence of his customary fitness and practice routines had removed some of the purpose from his life. He began to feel that, while he would never again achieve the playing level of his peak years, he should really assert himself and get into condition to play the best golf that he could at the age of forty-six.

All his life he had habitually swung from the tops of door frames, which required very strong fingers and an immediate visit to the bathroom afterwards because these ledges were invariably thick with dust and grime. Lately he had taken to carrying a gymnasium bar around with him, fitting it to door frames of hotels, ships and in his home. Both he and Toots would swing on this bar to stretch their muscles every time they passed through the door. He explained: "When we are kids we are always climbing, pulling or stretching. But once we're adults we slump and slouch over a desk, bench or steering wheel. The slouch is an unnatural posture. The spine gets stiff and set. It becomes susceptible to any sudden violence. My simple hanging exercise is all the correction you need. Just a few seconds with both hands, and then a few with either hand, a few times a day is all I do." But if he was to make a serious attempt to regain his old skills it would need more than stretching exercises on a gym bar. He spent ten weeks of the winter of 1952 doing exercises with an instructor who roused him from his bed at eight in the morning no matter how late he might have retired.

He won the first of his come-back tournaments, then pushed his luck by playing another the following week with rather less success and when he began to get dizzy spells in the third tournament he knew he had overdone it. His doctor ordered him off to the south of France for a rest, forbidding any more tournament golf that year and limiting him to occasional forays thereafter. Cotton's constant harping on physical fitness for the middle-aged in his newspaper and magazine writing was robustly challenged by the author Sir Compton Mackenzie on his 80th birthday who asserted that the way to attain old age was not to play golf.

J. H. Taylor, five times Open champion and still going strong at the age of ninety-one, was the first of many witnesses well stricken in years to defend a pastime which was known as 'the ancient and healthful exercise of the Golf' long before it became known as the royal and ancient game. Sir Compton was amused by the furore his remarks had caused and renewed his attack:

> I have always been influenced by what George Bernard Shaw meant when he said that 'The English got golf instead of wisdom.' Personally, I have always thought that in a game of golf there was just enough sport to ruin a good talk. And it should be remembered that the English put the Scots back by giving them port, and in return the Scots unloaded golf on the English for them to waste time with. But my point in all seriousness is that when a man reaches 57 or 58, which nowadays is middle age, and if he starts to worry about his golf, then he should give the game up. It is the menace of middle age, this worrying by men about their golf. I wonder sometimes, I really do, just how much all this swinging round has to do with the heart conditions of people we hear about. Far better to sit quietly, talk, read or watch television, I say. I haven't taken violent exercise for years.

For his part, Cotton went on preaching the virtues of golf as a guarantee of a healthy old age, and practising what he preached. He was to become a living proof of his theories. Among most sportsmen the legs go first but by the time Cotton emulated Sir Compton Mackenzie and celebrated his eightieth birthday those sturdy legs could cope with the five miles of walking involved in a round of golf without complaint. And the hands on which he had lavished a lifetime of exercise could still whip the club-head into the ball with the characteristic rolling action which had excited the admiration of golfers for sixty years. That, however, is rather getting ahead of the story.

At an annual dinner of the Professional Golfers' Association at Grosvenor House in London Cotton was one of the speakers and he took the opportunity to mount a pointed and well-founded attack on some of the association's reactionary attitudes and practices. Vociferous exception was taken to his remarks by his victims and shortly afterwards Cotton received a letter from the redoubtable Commander Roe:

> At the Executive Committee meeting held yesterday the question of your statement made at the annual dinner was considered and all members present were unanimous in deprecating your action there. This was a social function and should have been outside the business of the Association and it is earnestly hoped that you will write to our president, Lord Brabazon, apologising for making this statement in the midst of a social function.

Cotton's speech had been prompted by a growing resentment against what he considered to be interference and restrictions imposed on tournament players by club professionals who had little or no experience of tournaments. Strictly speaking there were no specialist tournament players at this time, since everyone held a club appointment, but there was a fairly well-defined group of professionals who concentrated on the growing programme of tournaments and left the day-to-day running of their shops to senior assistants. This was the beginning of a division of professional golf into two distinct careers, a split which was to be formalised after years of acrimony by the breakaway of the specialist players into the Tournament Players' Division of the PGA some twenty years later.

Cotton had once again fallen foul of PGA when he withdrew from the Dunlop 2,000 Guineas tournament at Sunningdale after playing a fine practice round of 69 because PGA officials would not give him an early starting time. Cotton had requested a change in his 2.18 p.m. starting time in order to honour a commitment to give a lecture to the Olton club in Birmingham that evening. He had already put the Olton club off twice. Cotton scratched from the tournament and was duly fined by the PGA for failing to give sufficient notice of his withdrawal.

The upshot was the formation of an unofficial players' committee, with Cotton as honorary secretary. This body was empowered to put forward the requirements of the players and to negotiate with the PGA for their adoption. They wanted fuller player representation on the executive committee and said that they would not accept invitations to play in any international match sponsored by the PGA unless they were satisfied with the selection committee and the choice of captain.

Once again Cotton was engaged in a mutiny, only this time he was not a lone voice but one of a powerful pressure group of Ryder Cup veterans. It took a number of meetings, both formal and behind the scenes, before the two sides composed their differences.

During the austere years after the war when the government was committing all its resources and energy to the reconstruction of the country, the Chancellor of the Exchequer, Sir Stafford Cripps, sent out an edict that all loss-making enterprises must be made profitable or closed down. Two well-loved icons of British life thereby fell under threat, the Moretonhampstead Manor and Gleneagles hotels which were owned by the British Transport Commission. A director of the Commission's hotel division and dedicated golfer, Sir Harry Methven, sought Cotton's advice about whether golf might provide a salvation. Cotton's energetic and imaginative response suggested that he might have made a successful politician.

Gleneagles, in its incomparable Perthshire setting in the foothills of the Grampians and with two fine James Braid golf courses, relied mainly on a wealthy golfing and sporting clientele, mostly from overseas, and so it had to be closed down during the winter. It could be made viable, as Cotton was informed, if enough business could be generated to extend its season by a month. Cotton was associated with the Saxone shoe company which sold a model called 'Gleneagles'. The solution was obvious, a Saxone-Gleneagles golf tournament involving Britain's finest professionals playing with wealthy amateurs. With the hotel and Saxone's contributing equally to the prize fund this Invitational Pro-Am Handicap event would fill the hotel for one week and proved to be a great success. Under Cotton's persuasion the Highland Brigade agreed to put back its jamboree for a month and the Fishmongers' Golfing Society also postponed its annual visit. The extra month was fully booked and Gleneagles was saved from the auctioneer's block.

Cotton's triumph had one painful consequence. At a gala dinner during the tournament his social and entrepreneurial obligations naturally required him to dance with the wife of the chairman of Saxone's. Much depended on the continuing goodwill of the company and Cotton was assiduous in his attentions to his partner. A trifle too assiduous, possibly? Who can make a judgment on such a subjective matter? Well, Toots could, for one. Suddenly, to the amazement of the rest of the party at the table, she leapt up, marched onto the dance floor and cracked him on the jaw with a right hander.

That at least was how the popular press reported the incident and there were plenty of precedents for Toots resorting to her fists, not to mention an umbrella on one occasion, for dealing with impertinent or officious creatures such as immigration officers, customs men and even police. In the interests of historical accuracy it must now be recorded that it was not a punch which stopped Cotton in his tracks on this occasion. It was, as Toots insisted many years later, a stinging, open-handed slap.

Cotton had never seen the Manor House at Moretonhampstead, on the edge of Dartmoor, until his visit some time later with Sir Harry Methven. He was enchanted by the old mansion and its short and sporty golf course. It was losing £6,000 a year and Cotton was told that he could buy it outright for £21,000. In later years when reflecting on a full and satisfying life, Cotton's one regret was his passing up of this opportunity of a lifetime.

His suggestion for restoring the fortunes of Moretonhampstead was to institute cheap golfing weekends, including first class rail travel. These 10-guinea weekend breaks proved so popular that they soon became over-subscribed and the hotel was forced to restore its normal tariff.

Cotton's help was again enlisted by the railway hotel group ten years later over the building of an hotel at St Andrews. This was a sensitive issue since it involved replacing the relatively unobtrusive railway station with a large and, as it turned out, ugly structure which violated the integrity of the compact, mediaeval city and marred its view for the approaching visitor.

The Royal and Ancient golf club was in favour of the hotel development and exerted its considerable influence. Cotton's role was to help enlist the support of the Prime Minister, Harold

Wilson. They corresponded on the basis of golfing pals and eventually the Prime Minister was able to convey the good news to Cotton: "I am very pleased that we have been able to give the green light to the hotel at St Andrews." He added a footnote: "Sorry the R and A is going to ban my putter." (The Prime Minister had resorted to using a croquet putter in his attempt, which had proved successful, to keep his score in double figures.) Wilson did not try to intervene in the acrimonious dispute which attended the debate over the banning of croquet putters but he did write to the R and A on another subject which proved to be a considerable embarrassment. He had received a letter inviting him to become an honorary member of the R and A and had replied warmly that he would be delighted to accept this honour. The club then had to write back deeply regretting that the Prime Minister had been the victim of a practical joker; no such invitation was contemplated by the Royal and Ancient golf club of St Andrews!

In 1956 the Cottons decided to take an extended golfing holiday in America. Golf had not yet emerged from its post-war stagnation in Britain. Only four new courses had been opened since the war, compared to 1,000 in the United States, and the pace was accelerating, with 500 courses under construction that year. Cotton greatly admired the dynamic of American professional golf and had a deep affection for his American contemporaries. He had not been back for eight years and wrote to Clifford Roberts, the autocratic chairman of the Augusta National golf club, saying that he would like to play in the Masters tournament for one last time. Roberts welcomed him fulsomely, telling the *Augusta Chronicle*: "We are very much complimented that he would make the trip over here for the express purpose of playing in our tournament." Contrast that attitude with the position today when the Masters is the hardest tournament in the world to get into, either as a player or a spectator.

Cotton had not touched a club for three weeks and had never played with the larger, American-sized ball. At the age of 49 his ability was not seriously impaired but he feared that his stamina would not hold up to four rounds of competitive play. He was right, finishing well down the field. But he learnt a valuable lesson. In one round he was paired with Gene Sarazen, one of the handful of players to have won all four of golf's classic championships. Sarazen told Cotton that he had never seen anyone hit the ball better and suggested that Cotton's results would improve if he learnt to use the wedge and pitch his shots into the watered American greens, instead of playing the chip-and-run shots which were called for by Britain's hard and undulating greens.

Playing almost daily with friends gave Cotton an opportunity to adjust to the bigger ball, practise the wedge shot and tone up his health. The following month he played in the White Sulphur Springs open tournament in West Virginia, a sentimental return to the scene of his earlier triumphs, and four solid rounds, three of them in the sixties, gave him a fifth place finish. He was thereby encouraged to try to qualify for the United States Open championship. He was the leading qualifier at the Westchester country club with rounds of 68 and 69 and greatly impressed the spectators.

Cotton employed his new pitch shot to devastating effect in a pro-celebrity tournament that week at Wykagyl golf club, winning the professional section with a 66 and the pro-am event with a 62. He made an unhappy start to the first round of the United States Open championship at Oak Hill golf club in upstate New York. He played with Jack Burke and Jimmy Demaret and at the end of the round Burke signed his card showing a 4 at the 18th hole where he actually had 5. Burke said: "It was all my fault, I have no one else to blame." Under the Rules of Golf it is a disqualification offence to sign for a score lower than the one actually taken but in this instance the United States Golf Association exercised its right in exceptional individual cases to waive the penalty of disqualification and impose a two stroke penalty.

What made this an exceptional individual case? Cotton never spoke of the incident but we may be sure that he made his views known at the time. Demaret had been a member of the American 1947 Ryder Cup team and was a close friend of its captain, Ben Hogan. That year, at Portland, Oregon, Cotton was the British Isles captain and he called attention to Rules irregularities by the Americans. Residual resentment may or may not have been a factor on this occasion but, at all events, Demaret refused to sign Cotton's card, also over a disputed score on the last hole. Whatever the grounds or motives for Demaret's objections, the committee rejected them and Cotton's score of 74 stood. Cotton had 72 in the second round, followed by 73, 75 for a share of seventeenth place. We shall never know exactly what happened on the 18th hole at Oak Hill, the only recorded incident involving an accusation against Cotton's propriety on the golf course. But a few general observations may be in order at this point. Great champions do not cheat and this is not necessarily because of their superior moral standards. The guarantee of their honesty is the fact that they are always under close scrutiny and they have too much to lose to contemplate indulging in the slightest bit of hanky-panky. But, human nature being what it is, lesser players quite frequently insinuate that a champion is less than meticulous in observing the finer points of golf law. Champions make honest mistakes of procedure, of course, such as Bobby Locke forgetting to adjust the position of his marker before replacing his ball in the 1957 Open championship, but there has been no recorded instance of a champion being penalised for cheating and the reason is because it simply is not worth it.

Cotton continued to play tournaments and matches, with some successes, in the fifties but he recognised that he would never win another championship and for him that meant his playing career was over. He went on playing out of loyalty to the sponsors, loyalty to his fans and because, like most successful golfers, he had become addicted to the drug of competition. But other interests and challenges in his life were becoming increasingly important to him.

Chapter 8

When the Cottons moved into 74 Eaton Square they entered into a style of life which might be described as their royalty-in-exile period. At Ashridge before the war they had entertained lavishly but, while he had single-handedly erased much of the working class stigma from the craft of the golf professional, there remained a taint of the parvenu about a professional golfer, no matter how famous and successful he might be. Indeed, to a certain type of snob, success and riches only made that taint worse. Cotton was sensitive to the infinite subtleties of social gradations, for he was himself a terrific snob who loved a lord almost as dearly as he revered a millionaire. By severing his professional connections with golf clubs Cotton felt more comfortable in his social ambitions.

In some ways he felt even more comfortable in France where he was held in higher esteem than at home. He spoke French fluently and both he and Toots relished the benign climate and the gracious atmosphere of the Riviera in winter when Parisian society moved to the Mediterranean coast. He therefore negotiated with the Société des Bains de Mer to establish a golf school in Cannes at the Mougins club. Although he was the 'Prof' this was not at all like an appointment as the professional to a British club. He engaged assistants to run the establishment and do the donkey work; his function was to give lessons to special clients, at his special rates, to play with the more notable visitors, most of whom were his personal friends, anyway, such as the Aga Khan, and to see that the place was run according to his exacting standards.

For many great players teaching is a chore and a bore, even if they can be persuaded to give a lesson at all, and when they do take a pupil out for an instructional round they assume that the pleasure of simply playing in the presence of a champion is enough to justify the fee. The teaching content of these rounds is perfunctory and often limited to an occasional hint, such as: "Why not try moving your right hand more on top of the club." That was never Cotton's way. He was the ultimate evangelist of golf. No matter who his pupil might be, or whether he was being paid or not, he become engrossed in the player's problems and determined to effect an immediate and dramatic improvement. It did not bother him a bit playing with a hacker; indeed, he was much more interested in the pupil's progress than his own golf and took great satisfaction at the reactions of delight and amazement when a 24-handicapper at last delivered the club-head solidly to the ball and for the first time in his life watched the ball soar into the distance. Cotton's snobbery was strictly an off-course condition. When he had a golf club in his hand he was a Samaritan anxious to help the needy.

As a foreigner and the daughter of the Argentinian equivalent of a feudal baron, Toots was immune from English class strife. She took people as she found them and as long as she found them dutifully respectful and duly appreciative of Henry's achievements she made no distinction between a prince and a newspaper hack. By the same token, anyone who incurred her displeasure was lacerated by the sharp edge of her tongue, regardless of social standing.

Eaton Square was to become more than an elegant and gracious home. It was to become a monument to Cotton's achievements. But this home was also a symbol for golf, an example of what could be achieved in the game from hard work, dedication and the unswerving pursuit of excellence. One important qualification must be attached to Cotton's snobbery. Unlike most snobs he did not ditch the friends of his earlier life, although both his brother, Leslie, and his sister, Dorothy, felt that he increasingly distanced himself from them, through the influence of Toots.

When it came to selecting staff for his new home Cotton naturally thought of his old caddie, Hargreaves, and his wife, Ivy. In the case of Ivy, the choice was entirely logical for she was an excellent cook, but Hargreaves had no experience or qualifications as a butler. What he did possess in full measure was an acute mind and a certain dramatic talent, as he had demonstrated in his role of straight man for Cotton's act at the Coliseum. Toots would soon kick him into shape. Hargreaves entered into the spirit of the job with great enthusiasm although he was quickly made aware that Toots would not tolerate his natural Sam Weller persona, a rough diamond who could be indulged because he was such a good fellow. He would have to acquire a polish as glossy as the one Toots demanded that he keep on the dining table.

The first time he laid that table for dinner, under Toots' supervision, it took him two hours before she was satisfied that he understood the precise spacing for every knife and fork and the exact disposition of the glasses. The cellar at No 74 reflected Toots' preferences, containing only champagne and fine claret, plus 150 varieties of liqueur. Both the Cottons were hospitable by nature and enjoyed entertaining their vast numbers of friends. Now that they were settled and no longer subject to the professional golf calendar, except when it suited his purposes, they were able to go out to parties, to the theatre and for Cotton to indulge his second sporting passion, cricket. He avidly followed the fortunes of Surrey, his boyhood heroes, and attended the Oval as often as he could.

The Hargreaves had their baby son, Robert, with them and Toots doted on the child. She bought all its clothes at Harrods and Hargreaves later recalled that the Cottons once came up with a proposition. They would not adopt Robert, the Hargreaves would remain in every sense the baby's parents, but the Cottons would take over complete responsibility for the child's upbringing and education. Ivy declined this offer and Robert grew up to be a greenkeeper.

While Toots busied herself going round the sale rooms buying the furnishings which met her exacting standards for the house Cotton found himself at a loose end on the days when he was not engaged for a round of golf. He decided that he needed a hobby and, inspired by the example of Winston Churchill, he decided to take up painting. Unlike Churchill, who took professional instruction in technique and obtained all the expert advice he could, Cotton determined that he would tackle painting in the same way that he had made himself a great golfer. He would learn through diligence, application and experiment. He had a shed erected behind the house, purchased paints and canvases and set to work. He was immensely prolific and enthusiastic and inordinately proud of the fact that his friends were prepared to buy his paintings. It did not matter to him if his pictures were sought only because of their novelty value; the fact of a sale meant that he was successful. He had little aptitude for drawing, as he demonstrated over and over again with his course designs, and he loved bright colours for their own sake, regardless of their suitability to his subject. He was a big brush man, as might be expected from his exuberant personality, and applied the paint thickly in bold swathes of colour. Toots, never one to suppress her feelings for fear of offending others, was scathing in her criticism of his efforts. She absolutely refused to allow one of his paintings into the house, remarking that they were totally unworthy to hang beside the van Dongen portrait of herself and her Goya sketches.

Cotton applied himself assiduously to painting a portrait of Toots, basing his approach on the style of van Dongen, but she was not flattered and would not entertain the thought of having it indoors. For his own self-portrait Cotton painted his hair green, his face orange and his lips purple. Asked why he had chosen these colours, he answered: "One of my odd whims." The painting was put on exhibition in Paris and auctioned for charity.

As a star of the music hall and a veteran of many wartime radio broadcasts such as *Hi, Gang!* and *Variety Playhouse*, Cotton was frequently invited to make guest performances on the air. He had long since graduated from the role of celebrity guest but was engaged as a professional performer who could handle his end of a scripted double act with the likes of Vic Oliver. Even in cold print the dialogue of those shows is evocative of the era:

> VIC: Good evening, Mr Cotton – I think we've met before.
> HENRY: Yes, about an hour ago in the car park.
> VIC: Car park?
> HENRY: Yes, you backed into my bumpers.
> VIC: I'm sorry. I should have shouted 'Fore!'.
> HENRY: Why? Did you hit three others?
> VIC: I hope you're not angry with me.
> HENRY: Of course not. It just supports my theory.
> VIC: What's that?
> HENRY: That it's not only on a golf course that you find wooden-headed drivers.

In November 1953 Cotton was invited to take part in the Royal Command Variety Performance at the Coliseum, doing a shortened version of his stage act of fifteen years previously.

Hargreaves, who by now had moved on and was working as a waiter, was recalled and they rehearsed for two days at the theatre, along with Anne Shelton, Max Bygraves, an ice-skating troupe which performed scenes from *Guys and Dolls* and *Paint Your Wagon*, and the inevitable Tiller Girls. The golf act went down well and Cotton finished by hitting a ball into the royal box, a touch of skill and showmanship which was loudly appreciated by the audience, including the Queen and the Duke of Edinburgh.

There is no doubt that Toots was in large measure responsible for Cotton's successes as a golfer. She motivated him, encouraged him, castigated him, consoled him and advised him. To a large extent Cotton was her creation and they were a true partnership. She followed him every step of the way in nearly every major event he played, only serious illness spoiling her one hundred per cent record, and in the early days before roped fairways this meant being literally at his side, a potent incentive for him to play his best at all times.

This habit of keeping him up to the mark continued when he finished playing and attended tournaments in his capacity as a contributor to the *News of the World* and other publications. This presented a problem at times because tournament golf had become more formalised and, while Cotton was entitled to press accreditation, Toots had no official status and was not therefore entitled to walk on the fairways.

It was a brave steward who challenged her at commercial tournaments but the Open championship was a different matter and the officials of the Royal and Ancient golf club were no respecters of persons, no matter how celebrated their husbands might be. Toots for her part was no respecter of officials of any kind. There was a brisk altercation at the 1962 Open and again the following year during the play-off between Bob Charles and Phil Rodgers at Royal Lytham and St Annes when Toots was banished behind the ropes among the common herd of paying spectators. Afterwards the R and A made it clear that Toots must not cause further embarrassment by attempting to walk behind the players on the fairways.

So at St Andrews in 1964 when the press corps went out in force to follow Tony Lema, the charismatic American who had arrived on the eve of the championship and had played only nine holes of practice on the Old Course, Cotton followed the play but Toots was nowhere to be seen. She was, however, present in a very real sense. After Lema completed each hole Cotton stayed back briefly and was observed using a small radio transmitter to relay a description of the play to Toots who was in their suite in Rusacks hotel. Some of the writers became intrigued by this performance and hung back while Cotton gave his private commentary in full detail. Toots always wanted more, demanding to know minutiae such as exactly where the ball had landed and the borrows on the putts. Cotton was slightly embarrassed at having his friends discover him being nagged through the ether.

Cotton enjoyed being lionised and exploited his fame with cynical amusement, although with his close friends he was always careful to affect a self-mocking tone in the English manner. When he attended Open championships he habitually spent much of his time in the press tent, until he was ready for lunch. He would then command one of his favoured writers to accompany him. On being asked where they were heading, Cotton would reply: "I am a legend and we can eat wherever we like." Whereupon he would stroll slowly along the line of corporate hospitality tents, signing autographs and acknowledging greetings. Inevitably, somewhere along the line an alert public relations official would run out and beg him to step inside because his company's guests would be thrilled to meet him. Cotton would graciously accept and, on being offered a glass of wine, would exclaim: "My goodness, are you doing things on the cheap? Surely there must be a bottle of champagne somewhere out the back for emergencies." A bottle would be procured from somewhere, often by the professional making a dash to the Bollinger tent a quarter of a mile away, and after greeting the guests Cotton would allow himself to be persuaded to force a little food down. "It is so nice to be remembered," he would remark. "People are so kind; I shall get quite fat but it would be churlish to reject such hospitality."

Although Cotton enjoyed this period of his life, and often recalled it later in nostalgic terms, it was not fully satisfying. Ever since he was a boy he had been fighting battles, the ritualised warfare of competitive golf and genuine campaigns of real life. Apart from the skirmishes of his domestic life, he had been a winner all the way. But contentment eluded him. He discovered that the satisfactions of life come from the fighting and that the elation of victory is followed by a feeling of deflation. He derived great comfort from his faith but his growing spirituality also served to put his achievement into perspective and prompted him increasingly to speculate on a life hereafter. At least he could take out a little insurance in that respect, hence his acquisition of a gaudy and rather badly printed parchment, signed and stamped with the papal seal, reading:

Most Holy Father
Mr Henry Cotton and family, humbly prostrate at the feet of your Holiness, beg the Apostolic Benediction and a Plenary Indulgence to be gained at the hour of death on condition that, being truly sorry for their sins, but unable to confess them and to receive the Holy Viaticum, shall at least invoke with lips or heart the Holy Name of Jesus.

Another manifestation of his intimations of mortality was his attitude towards his medals and trophies which he began to see as mere baubles. He wanted to leave a permanent memorial of his life and work. A great golf course would be suitable, one which made a statement about his philosophy of golf and which could bring enjoyment to golfers for all time. There were practical problems to be resolved, such as where it might be and who would pay for it, but one of his favourite aphorisms was: 'The opportunity of a lifetime must be seized within the lifetime of that opportunity.' He would just have to do what he could to contrive an opportunity.

Chapter 9

Cotton's name brought him a considerable amount of work as a golf course designer and his knowledge of golf strategy and stroke making, plus his vivid imagination, were invaluable assets in these enterprises. His grasp of the technicalities of course construction was less secure although he was never at a loss for an answer to a problem. His solution for one bumpy green was to order a steam roller onto it, thereby compacting the soil so badly that all the grass died and the green had to be rebuilt. He never subscribed to the dictum that the most important part of a golf course is under the surface and it is probably true to say that he considered his design work more as a source of income than as a vocation. Sometimes the design for a green which he handed to the contractor was a photograph of a famous hole torn from a golf magazine. When working in the places like Portugal where the construction crews were unfamiliar with technical drawings he used the old technique of making models of the greens in plasticine, for them to reproduce. He did his best work either on the site, where he could direct the operations, or in conjunction with an experienced contractor.

By the early sixties the Cottons were of an age when the English climate was becoming increasingly tiresome to them and their lavish lifestyle was exhausting their financial resources. They decided to find a place in the sun where they could live out their remaining years in comfort and tranquillity. Cotton heard of a golf project which sounded promising through a friend in Portugal. He made an approach to the developer and towards the end of 1963 he was invited to go to Portugal and appraise a piece of land for a golf course. He was shown a vast, flat, waterlogged area of paddy field about two miles inland from the Algarve coast near Portimao. Cotton took one look at this unprepossessing swamp and, anticipating a good fee, immediately declared: "Of course I can turn this into a beautiful golf course." Toots accompanied him on his next visit and was aghast at the prospect. She railed at him: "You must be mad. It is impossible to build a course here. Your reputation will be ruined." Cotton rejected her objections, although at that time he had no thought that this project might be an opportunity to create his memorial. The developer, John Stilwell, had chosen this site because the land was cheap and there was an abundance of water, an important consideration in a climate where a course needs a million gallons of expensive water every day. One vital element made the project feasible. The Stilwell family had a rice farm near Coimbra. Their farm workers had centuries of inherited experience of drainage and instinct guided their hands as they dug out a tracery of dykes, ditches and lakes with their wooden shovels. They worked to a tolerance of an inch without recourse to surveyor's levels. The site for Penina golf course seemed to rise from the ooze as the surplus water was drained away.

Thousands of eucalyptus trees, each absorbing 500 gallons of water a day, were planted. The spoil from the drainage work was used to elevate tees and greens and 350,000 hardwoods, conifers and flowering shrubs were planted. Cotton rose to the challenge. He fell in love with Portugal and the gentle Algarvians. This is where he would end his days and Penina would be his permanent memorial, a decision happily endorsed by John Stilwell who offered him a generous contract to become director of golf and legend in residence at the five-star golfing hotel. The work was completed in 1966 and two years later the Cottons took up residence, building themselves a splendid villa, Casa Branca, alongside the first tee.

Penina's reputation spread abroad. Cotton was the magnet for visits from his friends and tourists, many seeking the holy grail of golfing prowess from the Maestro. The hotel was the epitome of five-star luxury with the staff out-numbering the guests. The course matured quickly into a beautiful oasis of tranquillity where the golfers strolled down the fairways through avenues of towering trees. Penina became a haven for a wide variety of bird life never seen before in these parts. The Cottons were happier than they had ever been. In a sentimental moment he announced: "When I die I want to be buried standing up so that I can look out over my beautiful Penina."

In another sentimental moment he bought a donkey which he named Pacifico, based on the assurance by the farmer from whom he bought it that it had a tranquil nature, and had a pannier made for it which could accommodate two golf bags. Pacifico the caddie was a great success as an added tourist attraction and learnt to stand still while a shot was being played and not to walk on the greens. Cotton took a perverse delight in embarrassing women, mainly by telling really rancid jokes, often abetted by Toots, and Pacifico gave him an opportunity to indulge this penchant for making women squirm. When he was engaged to play a round with a visitor, frequently an American businessman seeking to polish his game against retirement to a condo on a Florida golf development, the wife often came along for the walk and to take the inevitable snapshots. On such occasions Cotton would stand alongside Pacifico and surreptitiously tickle its testicles, generating an impressive erection. Cotton once obtained even greater satisfaction from this ploy than the usual embarrassed departure of the wife to study the flowers. On this occasion a wife was stroking Pacifico's nose when she observed the tumescent results of Cotton's attentions and she shrieked in delight: "Look, Solly, he fancies me!"

The first tournament at Penina, the Algarve Open, was memorable for a mysterious act of sabotage. Cotton had built the course enormously long, about 7,400 yards. Each hole was furnished with lengthy teeing grounds, like the decks of aircraft carriers, or a progression of separate tees in some cases. This arrangement allowed maximum flexibility because the tee markers could be moved considerable distances according to the wind strength and direction, thereby enabling the holes to be played precisely the way Cotton had intended in all conditions.

For the first round of that Algarve Open an official of the Portuguese Open took advantage of that flexibility to set all the tee markers so far forward that Penina was emasculated. The professionals took full advantage of this generosity and murdered the course. Cotton was furious that his course had not been presented as a worthy challenge. He and the official had a blazing row on the first tee and the verbal exchanges degenerated into an exchange of blows. The greenkeeper, Manuel Nunes, separated them. The incident, much more characteristic of Toots than Cotton, did not end there. That night, around the witching hour, Toots crept out stealthily onto the course. Since there was a full field of some 150 competitors, play for the second round had to start early in the morning and the first group hit off from markers set at the extreme back limit of the teeing ground. It was the same story on the second hole; the markers were at the maximum distance the hole could be played. Every hole proved to be the same, played at the fullest possible length. In some cases the markers were so near the rear edge of the teeing ground that the golfers had to stand to the ball with their right feet halfway down the banking. Penina was a monster such as Cotton had never envisaged should be played. The scores soared.

At the time the phantom tee-mover was not positively identified. Suspicion naturally fell on Toots but her tongue could not be loosened. The other candidate for the moonlight sabotage was the disaffected official of the Portuguese Golf Federation, a suggestion vigorously propagated by Cotton. But he knew and disapproved of his wife's action, even though he appreciated her motive of ensuring that the professionals did not make a fool of the course again.

Cotton acted as referee for the Algarve Open and brought a certain measure of legal creativity to the job. One player hit his ball under a tree with low, spreading branches. The whole area was dotted thickly with molehills and the player duly sought relief from casts made by a burrowing animal. Having been permitted by Cotton to drop one club length away from an intrusive molehill the player pointed out that his ball now lay near another molehill. Cotton saw that the player could use this rule to work his way progressively clear of the tree and find himself with a clear shot at the green. He ruled that the player could take one more drop and that he would then have to play the ball, on a molehill or not, amid the encumbering branches.

Unlike the golf stars who succeeded him, who used ghost-writers to write their instructional books and reminiscences, including one of the most famous of them who could not be persuaded to read his own books, Cotton was a genuine working golf writer and most of his vast output of books and journalism was his own work. He wrote in longhand and needed very little editing. He had an innate understanding that the journalist's duty is to inform, to

With Archie
Compston at
RAC Club, Epsom
in 1929.

Below With Abe
Mitchell at the
1934 Open
championship.

Below right With
Walter Hagen.
Note the dropped
right shoulder.

Opposite With Lloyd Mangrum at Walton Heath in 1949.

Right On the beach at Deal after the War. Left to right: Lord Castlerosse, Henry Longhurst, Henry Cotton, Brigadier Critchley (playing) and Leonard Crawley.

Right Henry Cotton teaching limbless ex-servicemen in Roehampton.

Right Teaching in Monte Carlo with his patent ball dispenser.

Opposite With Nick Faldo at Penina in 1978.

I recommend

Penfold

GOLF BALLS

says

ONLY THE BEST IS GOOD
ENOUGH FOR ME ——
AND **YOU!**

PENFOLD PATENTED   For handicaps of 5 or better

For all good golfers   *Penfold* R.F. 126

GOLF BALL DEVELOPMENTS LIMITED
BROMFORD LANE · BIRMINGHAM, 8

The golf course plan in central France.

Opposite A 1948 advertisement.

Plasticine models of greens.
Below In Mar del Plata, 1930, with a
camel taking sand for bunkers.

The Open Trophy, 1948.

The 1953 Ryder Cup Team. Back row left to right: Harry Bradshaw, Bernard Hunt, Peter Alliss, Henry Cotton, Harry Weetman, Jimmy Adams and Eric Brown. Front row left to right: Max Faulkner, John Panton, Fred Daly and Dai Rees.

On stage at the London Coliseum in 1938.

A 1937 cartoon.

Doing a Cabaret at the Sporting Club in
Monte Carlo.

The first tee at Langley Park.

interpret and to entertain. Because of his experience, knowledge and lively mind he was well qualified to supply all three elements and he expressed himself in simple, basic English.

He never tried to compete with the giants of golf literature, such as Bernard Darwin and Henry Longhurst, both of whom he admired enormously. But he was thoroughly competent and could very well have made a successful career as a professional golf correspondent. He enjoyed the company of his raffish journalist friends, and not just for the sake of the publicity they could give him, and he was proud of his presidency of the Association of Golf Writers.

One of his closer golf writing friends was Mark Wilson, correspondent of the *Daily Express*, who habitually took his annual holiday at Penina in order to play golf with the Maestro. They had the usual prolonged arguments about handicap strokes and invariably the terms were that the loser should pay for dinner. This arrangement represented a typical Cotton deal, since he and Toots did not pay for their meals and their guests were half price whereas Wilson was liable for four full-price meals.

Cotton remained extremely competitive on the golf course for as long as he was able to swing a club and behind the banter of these jolly social rounds the desire to win was as strong as ever. On the first hole of their first match Cotton hit his approach shot to about five feet and while Wilson was sizing up the long putt he needed for a half, Cotton walked up to his ball and picked it up. Wilson demurred, pointing out that he had not offered a concession. Cotton replied: "The day you are born God gives you so many of those. At my age I am not wasting any of the ones I have left on you. I have nothing to prove to the likes of you, Wilson."

By this time Cotton had put on a considerable amount of weight, which he disguised in the evenings by wearing a florid kaftan. Toots tried to control his expanding figure by making him eat a hard-boiled egg before dinner, to kill his appetite, and indeed he did order sparsely. But he made an arrangement with the waiters for them to put cakes in the pockets of their aprons and when Toots was not watching he surreptitiously slid his hand down into their pockets.

Cotton's weight problem contributed to the natural tiredness of an old man who played golf every day and hated to miss any social activity in the hotel. He frequently took catnaps during dinner, his head sometimes reclining in his soup plate. Thus it was understandable that when he decided to write one last book, for by then he really needed the money, he should get his friend Wilson to do the donkey work. He was still conscientious about the book's content, and made notations and corrections on the draft, but it was a tape recorder work involving weeks of concerted toil by Wilson. As the deadline approached Wilson became more and more concerned about the title and he was immensely relieved when it finally came to him. He had found a photograph of Cotton raising his cap in acknowledgement of the ovation he received at Turnberry when he made his last, sentimental public appearance at the 1977 Open championship. He mocked up a book jacket with this photograph and the title 'Thanks for the Game' and showed it to the Cottons. Toots' reaction was typically forthright: "Rubbish!"

Wilson was in no mood to take that lying down. He was long past the stage of being deferential and was almost family to the Cottons. After all, when he hurt his back trying to outdrive Cotton he had been given an enema by the Cottons on doctor's instructions, with Toots making Henry stand on a chair while she, on the business end, urged him to hold the header-tank ever higher. Such experiences create a bond. He had earned the right to speak freely and did so, with some spirit, saying that unless Toots could come up with a better idea by the morning he would wash his hands of the project.

Toots spent the rest of the day in Cotton's study going through his enormous collection of photographs. Next morning she broke her usual routine of staying in bed until eleven o'clock while she telephoned friends around the world and came down to breakfast. She handed Wilson her version of the book jacket. It was a picture of Cotton embracing Pacifico the donkey with the suggested title: 'Kiss My Ass'. It was almost perfect, succinctly summing up with typical Cotton vulgarity his attitude since the day he refused to be caned at Alleyn's, his response to the reactionary attitude of the PGA and his brother professionals, his reply to the golf community which had reviled and rejected him for years, and his answer to the revolutionaries who were to hound him into exile. Unfortunately, the contents of the book were not concerned with such matters and the publisher settled for 'Thanks for the Game'. What a pity it was that Cotton never wrote the book for which that title would have been so appropriate. At least it remains ready at hand for the biographer who undertakes the task of writing Toots' personal story because that expression was her unspoken battle-cry, no less than his, throughout her combative life.

Cotton had just finished a lesson and was sitting in his office chatting with the pupil, a woman hotel guest who was due to fly home to London that evening, when two men entered. One of them was Francisco Jeronimo, the caddiemaster. Cotton did not recognise the other. They announced themselves to be members of the workers' revolutionary action committee and launched into a denunciation of Cotton. They accused him of abusing his terms of employment by exploiting and robbing the hotel staff, specifically by paying the boy caddies 15 cents each for the balls they retrieved from Penina's numerous lakes and waterways and then selling them at 75 cents, a fact that they had discovered when Cotton's secretary, Rosa Ghia, released the account books to the action committee. Cotton did indeed have a large cupboard full of reclaimed golf balls and these, the men announced, were summarily confiscated along with all his other stock in the shop. By this time Toots had joined them and she exploded with rage, the shouting match ending when she left to ring the British consul, who advised the Cottons to seek legal redress. Toots had little faith in the courts but she insisted that a lawyer be present when the action committee counted the stock of 36,000 golf balls. The process took four days.

Cotton was further accused of taking a ten per cent commission on villa sales in the cases where he had introduced the potential buyers, thereby appropriating money which rightfully belonged to the sales staff. Adding his ten per cent on green fees and 12 cents a day on every guest, the committee estimated that Cotton was 'profiteering through exploitation' to the extent of $250,000 a year.

Cotton was accused of having been autocratic towards the workers and a capitalist acquisitor ever since he had been at Penina. It was clear to Cotton that the two revolutionaries had gone around the hotel inviting the staff to denounce him, the usual practice during this period, and had cobbled together their accusations from a recital of petty grievances and jealousies. He sat calmly at his desk during this diatribe which ended with a demand that he vacate his office immediately, since it was needed as the headquarters of the workers' revolutionary committee.

Cotton was welcome to remain in his post at a salary of $1,000 a month and he could continue to charge for lessons. But he would have no other privileges since his profiteering had yielded him plenty of money to retain his villa and five servants. Cotton decided to resign. In that case, declared the revolutionaries, he must surrender the cheque books of all his bank accounts.

Cotton then announced firmly that the accusations were groundless, as they very well knew, since they were not privy to the terms of his contract with the hotel. He would give them the cheque book of his Portuguese account but their demand for the cheque books of his overseas accounts was a breach of international law and he would keep them. As for vacating his office, they were welcome to it but he would not leave until he had written a letter. The two men were taken aback by the authority of this response and stood there with the expressions of men whose bluff had been called while Cotton wrote his letter and addressed the envelope. As he and the woman he was teaching walked along the passage towards the lifts he gave her the letter and asked her to deliver it by hand without fail as soon as she reached London. She looked at the address, 'The Rt Hon Harold Wilson, 10 Downing Street', and protested that she could not just walk up and ring the bell of Number Ten. Of course you can, insisted Cotton, just pop it through the letter box.

That letter set in train a flurry of diplomatic activity which resulted in a *laissez passer* which guaranteed the Cottons unimpeded exit from Portugal. They packed what personal effects they could load into the car and drove to the border, taking the Vila Real ferry across the estuary to Ayamonte and booking into the local parador, one of the excellent hotels which the Spanish tourist authority create to preserve historic buildings such as castles and country houses.

Their first priority was to safeguard the contents and fabric of Casa Branca and a call was put in to Toots' daughter Chickie to fly down to Portugal immediately and install herself in the villa. As a visitor she would not be bothered by the revolutionaries; they were only interested in permanent residents. Since the villa belonged to permanent residents, albeit temporarily in exile, its status had to be changed. Cotton called Count John de Bendern in Lausanne, explained the predicament and asked him to meet them in Lisbon. Rooms were booked in the Palace Hotel. While the revolution had been entirely bloodless in the sleepy Algarve there had been some casualties among the foreign community in the north and at dinner they agreed to keep a low profile and stay put in the hotel. After dinner they said their goodnights and retired but the free-spirited de Bendern then got up and disappeared for a night on the town, a typical episode of the type which had long since caused Cotton to ignore the 'o' when referring to him by his formal title.

A lawyer was summoned and a lease of Casa Branca was formally assigned to de Bendern. The villa was now officially the dwelling of a non-resident and as such was immune from the attentions of the revolutionaries. That, at least, was the theory but Toots became increasingly concerned for the well-being of Chickie, all alone in Casa Branca, and the services of the faithful Count de Bendern were again enlisted.

The plan was that he should charter a small plane to fly him to the private landing strip behind the Penina hotel, in order to circumvent the currency restrictions in force at the commercial airports, and stay at Casa Branca as a bodyguard. Chickie drove in her hired Mini Minor to the airstrip at the appointed hour and waited, closely observed by a group of armed soldiers. The essential flaw in this cloak-and-dagger plan was that de Bendern could not bring himself to get onto an airplane until he had fortified himself with a few strong drinks. On this occasion, owing to the increased nervous tension inherent in the proposal of travel in a small and frail-looking aircraft, he thoroughly overdid his pre-flight tranquillising. As the plane drew to a halt Chickie was alarmed to see the door open and de Bendern fall out onto the runway. His briefcase burst open, scattering bundles of bank-notes. "It was," she recalled afterwards, "like something out of a James Bond film."

She gathered up the debris, both human and financial, pushed them into her car and drove off at high speed past the guards, whose interest in the proceedings had increased to a threatening degree, as the pilot made good his equally speedy exit.

As a bodyguard de Bendern proved to be more of an *agent provocateur*. After a short nap he insisted that he and Chickie would dine that evening in the Penina hotel. His response to the surly waiters lounging about in the otherwise empty dining room was to upbraid them in forthright terms: "You bloody fools! What is the point of taking over a hotel and then making it uninhabitable for guests? We're the only people who are going to give the hotel any custom this evening and you're doing your best to make us feel unwelcome. Jump about and let's have some proper service, starting with a bottle of champagne." The logic of this cheery homily struck home and some of the waiters, whom he had known for years, seemed relieved to revert to their accustomed role of polite servitude. Besides, de Bendern's generosity as a tipper had made him the most popular guest the hotel ever had. The head waiter, who announced himself as chairman of the workers' committee, alone persisted in addressing the two diners as 'comrade', and was roundly pilloried by de Bendern all evening.

At the parador Cotton relapsed into melancholy at the collapse of their fortunes and suffered a form of mental breakdown. Toots resolutely refused to be defeated by workers playing at being ruthless revolutionaries. She was enraged by their treatment of her husband but she was determined she could outwit them. She organised what amounted to a smuggling ring. Every day Chickie drove to the border, an innocent tourist visiting her mother. The border guards got to know her and after a while even stopped searching her handbag. She never had anything of consequence on her. In fact Chickie was systematically taking important family papers into the safety of Spain, property deeds, insurance policies, contracts, bank statements and so on, hidden in a magazine. The only mishap was that she somehow contrived to lose Toots' will on her travels.

News of the Cottons' enforced exile had been widely reported in the papers, as a result of which one of his oldest and closest friends, Pierre Crokarte, got in touch with him. Crokarte, a Belgian mining engineer, had first met Cotton at Waterloo and had been a regular visitor to Penina. He now lived at Sotogrande, a few miles up the road from Gibraltar, where the wealthy American developer, Joe McMicking, had created a major housing development with a golf course and polo ground, very expensive and very exclusive. McMicking had recently built a second golf course. Sotogrande New as it was then called (now Valderrama) had no professional and Crokarte felt sure that Cotton would be the ideal man. He invited the Cottons to come and stay with him. Once installed, Crokarte initiated negotiations with McMicking. The upshot of these discussions was that McMicking suggested Cotton become director of golf at the new course and help to put it on the map. Toots, ever alert to the practicalities, quizzed him about fees and where they might live. McMicking was more than generous in his offer. The Cottons could have one of the apartments by the golf club. Toots asked about its size. McMicking started to describe the apartment and then stopped, reading Toots' mind and remarking that it would not be nearly big enough for them. He would knock two apartments into one for the Cottons. The deal was struck.

The episode of exile from Portugal was the low point of Cotton's life. Toots' dominating personality carried him through the ordeal, just as it had sustained him in his golf career. There were precious few moments of light relief although months later he found wry amusement in the form of a picture postcard of Sugarloaf mountain from Rio. It read: "Things have not gone well for me since I arrived in Brazil. I know you to be a fair and generous man and I shall ever be in your debt if you could use your great influence to secure me employment at Penina as I am greatly desirous of returning to Portugal." The signature meant nothing to Cotton so he made enquiries. This request for help was from the man who had spied on him and denounced him in his own office in company with Jeronimo.

Chapter 10

*T*he Cottons settled comfortably into their new life in Sotogrande. They had a spacious apartment at the golf club and quickly made many new friends among the international community. Old friends who had habitually taken holidays at Penina, such as Joe Carr and his family, simply changed their routines and went to Spain to play golf with Cotton. He kept busy with lessons and playing the course, which is now called Valderrama, and he was greatly cheered when he was reunited with his caddie, the donkey Pacifico, which had been spirited across the border by a devious route and transported to Sotogrande. Pacifico did not long survive in Spain. The only stabling available was with the polo ponies which were, of course, all fillies. This arrangement was immensely exciting for Pacifico, too exciting as it transpired. Cotton insisted that Pacifico died with a smile on his face from excessive sexual stimulation, or as he put it, "The mortal combination of a dicky heart and a hearty dick."

It was not long before Cotton himself was in the wars. He slipped on some steps and cracked a rib, nothing too serious according to the diagnosis of the local doctor. It certainly looked serious. He was a ghastly grey colour and kept sliding into a stupor during which he could not recognise even his closest friends. Toots called his doctor in Paris and described the symptoms. She was advised that it certainly sounded more serious than a cracked rib and that he should have an expert examination. Toots broke her lifetime rule against flying and chartered an air ambulance to take them to Paris. In addition to three broken ribs, Cotton had ruptured his spleen, a lung had been punctured and he was suffering from pneumonia. It was several anxious weeks and three major operations before he was fit enough to return to Sotogrande.

His unhappy experience had taken the sheen off their Spanish interlude. Cotton pined to return to Penina. He had declined an invitation from the Royal and Ancient golf club to play in the Open championship of 1977 at Turnberry on the fiftieth anniversary of his first Open but Toots insisted that it would give him a new interest in life and restore his morale. He agreed somewhat reluctantly, but as soon as he had made the decision he set about getting himself fit and worked on his game with enthusiasm. He was determined to show the world that Henry Cotton could still play golf.

His playing companions were Arnold Palmer, whose example had elevated American professional golf into a major spectator sport in much the same way as Cotton had in Britain, and the greatest player in the history of Irish golf, Christy O'Connor, both past their prime but still active competitors. Cotton's undoing was the funereal pace of play. At seventy he was still capable of returning a respectable score when playing at the brisk clip of his era. He was himself considered to be a slow player by his contemporaries, his meticulous preparations sometimes causing a three-ball to take three and a quarter hours to complete 18 holes. But to be out on the golf course for something over five hours was quite outside Cotton's experience and beyond his physical capacity. The wearisome waiting on every shot sapped his energy and his concentration and he scored 93. Even so, the expedition fully justified Toots' insistence that he should play. Just being back in his old environment, among golfers and his old friends, restored Cotton's zest for life and he determined to return to Portugal.

The revolution had run out of steam and the hotel, with hardly any guests for two years, had fallen deeply into debt. A sign was needed that life was back to normal on the Algarve and John Stilwell told Cotton that he would be most welcome to return. The traumas of exile and his accident had markedly aged Cotton, he was tired and wanted nothing but to return home. When one of the Penina waiters, a leading light of the workers' action committee who took a sullen delight in his immunity from dismissal, rudely upbraided Cotton for not speaking in Portuguese, he bit back the reprimand that would have been forthcoming two years previously. He simply turned to his companion and remarked: "I want to live out my days in peace. If there are any disputes let them be resolved on the golf course." It was just as well that Toots was not present on that occasion for both the waiter and Cotton would have been roundly chastised for their behaviour.

It soon became clear to the Cottons that there would have to be changes in their routine, and far more fundamental changes than simply refusing to go anywhere near his old office which held such bitter memories for both of them. The fortune which Toots had inherited had gone, eroded by the rapacity of the Peron regime in Argentina, swingeing taxation by the post-war governments in Britain, and by their philosophy of living for the day, which meant on a style far beyond the income which Cotton himself generated. The important thing for both of them was that they should be able to go on entertaining their friends in lavish style. Human contact was more precious than bricks and mortar and Casa Branca with its five servants was too much of a drain on their dwindling resources. The villa was sold and some of the more valuable pieces of antique furniture sent for auction. Cotton even made enquiries in the golf collecting world about what his memorabilia, such as his trophies and medals, his considerable library of golf books and old clubs, would raise.

They moved into a penthouse apartment in the hotel. They told everyone that they were broke but the term was relative. It may have been a come-down from a grand mansion in Belgravia but to most people their new situation represented a dream of luxury. They had plenty of room to receive groups of the size which they had previously entertained for dinner at Casa Branca and it was no great hardship, after the preliminary drinks, to go downstairs to the dining rooms. In some ways it added to the sense of occasion for the Cottons and their guests were always given the full VIP treatment by the hotel staff when on public display, even if some of the waiters were less than totally respectful in private.

The tradition of the annual visit by the golf writers and their wives, along with gala dinner and cabaret, continued. This curious ritual had grown out of the Cottons' early custom of hiring a coach to take the party to Loule, in the foothills of the Monchique mountains, for a riotous evening at a fish restaurant. As the red wine and the pernicious local liqueur, *medronho*, took its inevitable toll of civilising restraints, Cotton in his ribald way commanded that the wives should stand up in turn and tell a dirty story. A few of them attempted to comply but there were mutinous mutterings and broad agreement that if the group were required to sing for its supper it would do so on its own terms, in close harmony and after proper rehearsal. So the cabaret was instituted the following year in the hotel and proved very popular. A surprising amount of musical and comic talent was unearthed. Toots, who allowed herself the luxury of saying exactly what she thought on every occasion, completely unwound and entered into the spirit of the occasions although she reverted to type at a formal dinner when one of Cotton's important sponsors made him a presentation of a beautifully carved rocking horse, one quarter scale. As he was making his presentation speech the piercing voice of Toots interrupted his solemn words: "Henry! You're not taking that thing upstairs!"

All his career Cotton was diligent in dropping notes of congratulation and gratitude to his friends and benefactors, just as he urged his young pupils should be. He had a cavalier way of addressing his notes, which tended to be vulgar and doubtless a source of amusement to the postal workers. The author once received a ribald card from Portugal addressed simply: Dobers, Pratts Bottom, England. The television journalist, Sandy Gall, a frequent visitor to Penina with his wife, Eleanor, and family, were second and third generations of friends of the Cottons for Mrs Gall's father was the surgeon who saved Cotton's life when he operated on him for appendicitis, a condition which would have been much less serious if Toots had not insisted that he stopped bellyaching about his bellyache and finished the tournament he was playing. Sandy Gall was the recipient of one of Cotton's famous notes in 1987, addressed to Mr Hole-in-One Gall. "What a bloody wonder! A hole in one!! What can be expected next!!! You are really getting too big for your shoes. I suppose Eleanor did not care, too, but I do! Bravo. You really must tell 'How I done it'. Hope we can have a laugh again soon."

Soon after Christmas in 1986 Cotton sat at his desk and wrote the following:

Goodbye Toots.

Until we meet again, my darling. I never thought you would leave me so soon, on Christmas morning at 9 a.m., and so suddenly too. We miss you dreadfully but are relieved that you passed away as easily and painlessly. The good Lord must have wanted you badly. I hope that you are happy in His care. You have lived for me entirely, for long years. I hope you understood that I lived for you. You were a great person, your life was spend guiding and helping me. Fate threw us together over 50 years ago and then we made our way together, not always easily, pioneering my career, with no precedent. We have many friends everywhere who knew and loved you and who realised you were different, a one and only.

We had a beautiful 24th of December – lunch, nine holes of golf on a sunny afternoon. She drove the cart. I walked and rode with her. Mass at 6.30 p.m. which she looked forward to, then dinner. She enjoyed her evening meal. Bed at 10.30 p.m. Then at 8 a.m. I took the dog out for half an hour. Back in the room at 8.30. I ordered breakfast. We exchanged presents and cards. Chickie, her daughter, was there and we talked about dressmakers. Suddenly she said: "I can't breathe." "You must have a cold" I said. Then she got out of bed seeking, I thought, air. Three times she hopped out of bed, alone, with no help. As I was putting extra pillows behind her she said: "Call the priest and the doctor. I am going to die." Rev Father John Creaven S.M., a golfer too, who was with us at Penina over the holiday saying mass daily for our English-speaking guests, rushed to the room and heard her say again "I'm dying." The young doctor, wife of the assistant manager, Christopher Stilwell, arrived just in time to hear her say once more: "I'm dying." And then she just closed her eyes and went. I still can't believe it.

My Toots was born with a unique sense of justice and fought hard to obtain it. I taught her to play golf and with her determination and courage she got down to an LGU 8 at Ashridge G.C., Herts, her limit, I reckon, as she was too frail to be a tigress. Before the war in 1937, when we were on a trip in Austria, she won the Ladies' Open championship, after being 5 down with 9 holes to play in the 36-hole final. I told her she was 'yellow' for she was not trying as she would normally. This stung her, as intended, and she tried on the last 9 fit to burst to prove me wrong. And she did, she won 1 up. I suffered of course, after that and got the 'I told you so' treatment but I enjoyed my 'triumph'.

After the war, when the tough British climate drove us on doctor's orders to seek a warmer climate, we went to the south of France, to Monaco first, then to Cannes. Her health, which was poor during the war years, recovered and she used to amuse herself with golf and with regular visits to the casino where she played for little money. But when her system failed, for she was always trying systems, and she lost she was sorry for herself and said meekly, when asked what happened, "I lost xx francs. Can we afford it?" We managed.

There is such a gap in my life at present that I am lost but will try to carry on as she would have wished. Despite the usual family disputes, usually my fault, we had a great and happy life together. Perhaps we can carry on later. Who knows? She lies next to her elder daughter, Nelly, in the graveyard of the church at Mexilhoeira Grande where there are two more plots waiting.

The purchase of Penina by Trusthouse Forte in 1986 marked a revival in the hotel's fortunes. Lord Forte and his family had been close friends of the Cottons for many years. There were many similarities between the two men. Both had started with nothing and had been driven by inner demons to scale their individual Everests, Cotton as Britain's greatest golfing icon and Charles Forte as the creator of an international hotel group. Both had achieved their successes through phenomenal hard work and by laying down their own ground rules rather than following convention. Their mutual affection and respect had survived a brief contretemps of Cotton's making in 1981 when Forte cancelled a golf date. It is commonplace among sportsmen who are constantly in demand for interviews and whose every word is faithfully reproduced in the newspapers to come to believe themselves to be oracles on any and every subject. In this field of instant omniscience, as in so many other ways, Cotton was a voluble pioneer. He had been haranguing Forte during their games of golf on how to run the hotel business and for this reason Forte concluded it would be better if they did not play together. If the situation had been reversed, with Forte nagging Cotton to change his grip, the outcome would have been the same. But more storm clouds were over the horizon, billowing from the over-heated ambition of the secretary of Cotton's lifelong adversary, the Professional Golfers' Association, Colin Snape.

Snape and his family had regularly enjoyed holidays as guests of Penina and he saw a potential for mutual benefits for his association, the hotel and himself. He was commissioned by

Trusthouse Forte to analyse the Penine golf operation and he looked around the property, assessing the layout, the staff and equipment. His report called for a comprehensive revision of the course, its conditioning, its staffing, its machinery and the creation of a continental headquarters for the PGA. For all its inaccuracies and blindingly obvious statements, such as drawing attention to the poor condition into which the course had fallen, the report was thorough, fully costed and generally plausible. Rocco Forte, who had taken over executive control of Trusthouse and who knew all too well the course needed attention, gave the go-ahead initially for the parts of the report which called for a thorough reconditioning.

The first Cotton knew of all this was the arrival of Snape with David Thomas, the golf course architect, and a construction crew. He was perplexed that Snape and his party deliberately avoided him, limiting themselves to the barest civilities when they met. Then, to his amazement and distress, he observed from his apartment windows that the course on which he lavished his attentions for twenty years and into which he had built the definitive statement of his golfing philosophy, was being fundamentally changed. Mature trees which were critical to his design strategy were felled; bunkers were re-shaped and enlarged to make it essential for the golfer to fly approach shots onto the green through the air on holes where Cotton had deliberately planned a chip-and-run option; new bunkers were added which distorted his basic concept. Cotton was deeply hurt that he had not even been consulted and felt that he had been betrayed by his friends. The press expressed outrage at what was being done to Cotton's masterpiece and about the way in which it was being done. Rocco Forte robustly defended the work by claiming that no significant changes were made in the design of the course; it was simply being put into good condition. For proof of this contention he produced reports on the work programme which he had received from Penina. Cotton gave chapter and verse of the changes in progress and how the playing character of different holes was being fundamentally altered. Work stopped and in some cases changes were restored.

This reversal was too late for Cotton. Hurt and disillusioned, he left Penina, telling the *Algarve News*: "I have been insulted and my work belittled." There was nothing left for him in Portugal. He went to live in London with his stepdaughter, Chickie, his memories and his greatest solace, his two dogs, Dolly the stray he adopted in Portugal, now blind, and her guide, Trixie.

In December that year, 1987, Cotton was admitted to King Edward VII's Hospital for Officers. He was in skittish mood with the nurses, teasingly quizzing them on the details of their love lives and plotting little surprises. One of them entered his room to find him with an arrow piercing his head and sheets drawn up under his chin by three enormous, hairy paws. One serious subject engaged his attention. He had received a letter from 10 Downing Street informing him that he had been nominated for a knighthood and enquiring whether he would accept such an honour. His initial response was that the title would mean that he would be overcharged in restaurants. He discussed the offer with Chickie and they both understood very well how Toots would have reacted; she would have considered the knighthood to be too little and too late. On reflection Cotton realised that, if he declined, his rejection might inhibit other honours being awarded to golfers. For the sake of the game to which he had devoted his life he decided to accept and he looked forward to receiving the accolade because he had been a staunch royalist all his life, especially since he had enjoyed the friendship and golfing companionship of the golfing dukes, of York and Windsor, later to become King George VI and Edward VIII.

The blood clot which had threatened his life had been dispersed and Cotton was convalescent, albeit suffering from a cold, when he died peacefully. His body was returned to Portugal and on Boxing Day he was buried alongside Toots and Nelly at Mexilhoeira Grande. Buckingham Palace announced that although he had not received the accolade symbolically conferring the knighthood he should be known posthumously as Sir Henry Cotton.

EPILOGUE

On March 16, 1988, a memorial requiem mass was held for Sir Henry Cotton at the church of the Immaculate Conception, Farm Street. The address was given by Lord Deedes, as follows:

Because he so loved golf, it seems to me right to begin with a word or two about Henry Cotton's finish in the 1937 Open at Carnoustie; for it tells us a great deal about the extraordinary man we are here to remember. It was arguably the greatest of his three Open victories, achieved against the best of America's

Ryder Cup and the worst of weathers.

With two shots in hand, he took a 3-iron to the 72nd green. The main threat to him was the fence on the left, which was out of bounds. Long after his victory, Henry Cotton was asked what passed through his mind at that moment. "Boy," he said, "I just aimed it out of the heel."

Now of course that reminds us that as a striker of the ball he stood alone – for lesser mortals would probably have shanked it. But it says much more than that. It illustrates a self-confidence, a strength of mind, which set Cotton's life a little apart from all the rest.

From quiet home and small beginnings out to the undiscovered ends, the milestones in Henry Cotton's life were marked by a rare strength of mind. We observe it in that early decision to explore America – to learn more about a lifestyle which seemed to give them an edge over us. And then, defiantly, to shape his own lifestyle: silk shirts from Jermyn Street, suits from Savile Row, the best restaurants . . .

I say 'defiantly' because one has to belong to my generation to realise that it was not as easy then as it may seem now. Our class system – what Shakespeare called 'degree' – was very strong in the days when Henry Cotton turned professional at 17. A professional golfer, playing with the Prince of Wales, could still not enter the clubhouse to join him for a drink.

It called for an heroic character; it called for great strength of mind – as well as blistered hands – to seek pre-eminence in that world then. Not only to seek pre-eminence, but to *change* it – they stood up, when he walked into the Savoy Grill.

Every British professional golfer since has been heir to an estate which Henry Cotton created and bequeathed to them. He did not do it all here. At the back of his mind when he went to Waterloo there lay the thought that a prophet is not without honour – save in his own country. Golfing visitors were treated better than our own kind!

By some accounts, his was a lonely voyage to the stars. And certainly, as one writer has put it, he often 'walked the fairways in mental isolation, retired into his own ivory tower'. But he was not of course altogether alone because, after his winter voyage to the Argentine, there was Toots.

When I think of Toots, I think of the story Laddie Lucas told me of Henry's agonising final round in the memorable Championship of 1934. You may recall the setting. 132 for the first 36 holes, a safe 72 in the third round, and then – never granted the strongest of digestions – he ate something that disagreed with him.

So, in the final round, he was 40 to the turn, followed by three 5s in a row – then a long steadying putt at the 13th. On the 14th tee he says to Toots, "I think my legs are giving way; I can't go on." As Lucas puts its so expressively, "She must have said something quite severe to him . . . " For there was no more talk of his legs. He went on to that victory which ended the long, lean years.

That was a blessed partnership, of which it can be said, that when she died, and for him the sun went down, it went down in a cloudless sky.

Men of such determination and with such strength of mind may well appear austere to those who do not know them well. But there was always a strong streak of humour in Henry Cotton – he must surely have needed it to appear, as I saw him, at the Coliseum in 1938 with a 15-minute act – and in the same bill as Nellie Wallace.

On the course, he was – and properly – a severe opponent. At the dinner table he was an engaging companion, happiest talking golf, but well-versed on cabbages, kings and sealing wax. He was slightly dotty about animals, invariably kind to and interested in the young. And for all that intensity, all that strength of mind, he yet believed that there was more to life than golf.

In his final hours, he was gladdened by the earthly gift of a knighthood; but, as one who believed in his religion, he was more humbly interested in what might await him on the far side.

He belongs to that small company who were the pioneers of this century. Henry Cotton lived and worked for much of his life outside these shores, and now lies buried besides Toots in Portugal's Algarve. Yet he quintessentially belongs to England. He belongs to our history of the 20th century.

He had a philosophy, as well as a matchless swing. We find a clue to it in a few lines he quotes from an unknown author at the start of one of his books, *My Golfing Album*: "Whether 70 or 16, there is in every being's heart the love of wonder, the sweet amazement at the stars and the star-like things and thoughts,

the undaunted challenge of events, the unfailing appetite for –
what next, and the joy and the game of life." Just so.

"Never forget," the poet Rilke said to his wife as he lay dying,
"never forget that Life is magnificent." And it is through the
experience and example of someone like Henry Cotton that we
learn the truth of that.

PART TWO

Cotton the Golfer

Chapter 11

Any attempt to put a player into historical perspective must take into account the structure of golf during his career. Up to a period well into the second half of the twentieth century there were very few formal tournaments in Britain. There was no distinction between a golf professional and a professional golfer; every pro had a club appointment and his first responsibility was to be present at his club at weekends to play with the members. For this reason such tournaments as there were, including the Open championship, were arranged to finish on a Friday night. Pros supplemented the meagre diet of perhaps six tournaments a year with challenge matches against each other, either singly or in pairs. The better-known players were mostly able to find backers to put up the challenge prize but the lesser lights who took up a challenge had to play for their own hard-earned money.

Willie Park Junior maintained a standing advertisement for many years in *Golf Illustrated* challenging all comers to a head-to-head match for £100. After becoming the first English professional to win the Open, in 1894, J. H. Taylor issued a challenge to play any man in the world for £50 a side. The canny Scot, Andra Kirkaldy, took up the challenge and salvaged Scotland's pride, winning by one hole. Some of these matches created enormous public interest, attracting as many as 20,000 spectators. So in assessing the place in golf history of a champion such as Harry Vardon it is not enough simply to count his tournament and championship victories, impressive as those totals were. Only by giving due weight to his unprecedented record in challenge matches can we get a complete picture of his dominance of the world of golf.

Cotton was the last major figure of British golf from the challenge match era, although he pioneered what was to become the European Tour by competing in continental national championships and playing in every European golfing nation, in addition to the handful of British tournaments each year.

Cotton was considered by his contemporaries to be temperamentally more suited to stroke-play than the hand to hand combat of matches. Even so, he collected some notable scalps. He beat Jack Smith over 72 holes for £50 in 1928 and the following year he beat the better-known Horton Smith, the American prodigy who won eleven tournaments in his first year as a pro. Smith was at a considerable disadvantage in this match because of the condition that he must play with hickory-shafted clubs. A return match was arranged the following year and by this time Cotton had converted to steel-shafted clubs and Smith was able to use his normal set. Cotton won that set, too.

In 1933 the American Ryder Cup team was narrowly beaten at Southport and Ainsdale but two members of that visiting side, Craig Wood and Densmore Shute, tied for the Open championship at St Andrews, with Shute winning the 36-hole play-off. Shute and the American team captain, Walter Hagen, stayed on in Britain to play exhibitions and challenge matches and so it was a considerable feather in Cotton's cap when he beat Shute 6 and 5 in a challenge for £500, put up by his friend, Sir Emsley Carr, editor of the *News of the World*, at Walton Heath. Following that notable victory the American golf press voted Cotton the Golfer of the Year.

Emboldened by his success over the Open champion, Cotton issued a challenge to the formidable Hagen, undoubtedly the world's leading professional. The match was played at Ashridge over two rounds and Cotton held a one-stroke lead after 27 holes. Hagen asserted himself over the closing stretch to win that one by 3 and 2. Shortly afterwards Cotton moved to Belgium and challenged Hagen to a return match, seeing this as an excellent way to prove himself in front of the Royal Waterloo members as well as a chance to get his revenge. In true Cotton fashion he publicised the coming clash as thoroughly as he could and crowds flocked from all over Belgium to watch the clash of the titans. The only thing missing was Hagen himself. The debonair American had a reputation for making a dramatic last-minute arrival on the tee, once in his dinner jacket after an all-night party, but when there was no sign of him an hour before the scheduled start of the match Cotton was really worried. He telephoned the Savoy and the best hotels in Brussels, the places he felt most likely the companionable Hagen might be dallying. In fact Hagen had set out in good time but his flight to London ran into a massive thunderstorm and was diverted from Brussels to Antwerp. Hagen telephoned Cotton and told him of the delay, assuring him that the flight would take off for Brussels as soon as the weather cleared. With this assurance, Cotton managed to entertain the gallery and Hagen arrived just in time to save having to return the gate money. With his usual grace, Hagen apologised for his late arrival and described his adventurous trip to the gallery, restoring the mood of good humour and keen anticipation for the golf. In the first round Cotton set a course record of 66 to Hagen's 67, a remarkable enough performance after such a journey. Cotton scored 67 in the second round to win a famous victory by 6 and 5.

Those victories over Shute and Hagen were valuable lessons in Cotton's education as a golfer, not in terms of his technique which by now was as effective as anyone's, but as reassurance. He had comprehensively beaten the best player in the world, and the reigning Open champion, and he had gained the confidence needed to become a champion in his own right.

Five years later, after Cotton had duly achieved his destiny as a double champion, a young player arrived on the scene with no less confidence in his ability to take the world of golf by the tail. Bobby Locke had turned professional after winning every honour his native South Africa had to offer, including the national Open championship. He was by nature a gregarious young man with an outgoing personality and a skittish sense of fun. His good nature was put to the test when he turned pro because he immediately ran into the worst aspect of professional golf. It is a hallmark of a great golfer that he relishes competing against other giants of the game but all professional golfers' associations are run along broadly democratic lines and this means that the policy-making is dominated by the majority. And they, by definition, are the second and third raters, men who want the prize money spread down the field to reward their incompetence and who resent newcomers encroaching on their preserve. So Locke was refused membership of the Transvaal Professional Golfers' Association until he had been a pro for two years.

Since he proposed to make his living as a player and had no interest in working in a shop, he sailed for Britain in company with his manager, Len Oates, and another young golfer, Sid Brews. Their plan was to play the Open and a challenge match against Cotton and Reg Whitcombe, hoping that they would do well enough to break down the barriers of the British PGA's five-year eligibility rule.

Golfers have used psychology to overcome their own mental shortcomings and to exploit the weaknesses of opponents ever since the game began but Locke was the first to make a study of the subject. His documentation of how to read signs of apprehension in a match-play opponent, and how to exploit them, stands comparison with anything published by professional sports psychologists. Learning from experience, he realised that his brisk, happy-go-lucky nature needed to be modified for golf. Getting to his ball too quickly and having to wait for his turn to play impaired the shot. Responding to greetings from the gallery unsettled his concentration. Having analysed such problems Locke invented for himself a special persona for golf.

In time he would develop the idea further, creating a uniform for his golf of white cap, tie tucked into white shirt, blue plus-fours and white shoes. But initially he concentrated on mastering his new personality for golf. He assumed a deadpan expression, never betraying disappointment or delight. He forced himself to walk slowly with a measured tread, always up the centre of the fairway so that he would be as far as possible from distractions in the gallery. He schooled himself to follow a set routine for every shot, most noticeably with his unvarying putting drill of inspecting the line from both directions, taking his stance, making two practice swings and then inching forward and striking the ball. As a result he always looked composed, always played well within his physical and emotional limits. The message his demeanour and deportment conveyed to the other contestants was that he was unflappable and serenely confident in his own abilities. He was probably the surest putter of his or any other era. It would be difficult to imagine a bigger contrast between the gravitas of the Arthur Darcy Locke on the links and the skittishness of the Bobby Locke who sang witty ditties to his own ukulele accompaniment and who went off on nefarious escapades with Max Faulkner.

And in time even he seemed uncertain about which was the 'real' Bobby Locke.

In his baptism of British golf at Sandwich for the 1938 Open championship Locke made a solid start and was only three strokes off the lead after two rounds. Then came the great gale of the final day. The ten-stone stripling was blown off balance by the ferocity of the winds which lacerated the tents and he finished eleventh. The British PGA informed Locke that he was not eligible to play in the Irish Open championship and there was considerable hostility among the membership when his entry was accepted. Cotton was the star attraction at Portmarnock and in the first round Locke seemed to have played himself right out of it with an opening 80, and that only by dint of an eagle at the last hole. His second round 73 left him nine strokes behind the leader, Cotton. Locke holed a fifteen-footer at the 18th for a third round 69, the first player in the field to break 70 and challenge for the £200 bonus put up by a Dublin sportsman. Cotton had 73 for a five-stroke lead to take into the decisive round. Locke's phenomenal putting, one putt on each of the last four greens for four birdies gave him a 70 and a total of 292. Now he had to wait. Cotton's play of those last four holes was a sad contrast. The one weakness in his game was a slapdash quality in his putting which made for erratic performances on the greens. Some days he putted well but he was always vulnerable on the greens, never more so on those closing holes at Portmarnock. Over the stretch where Locke had taken a total of four putts Cotton required ten. That was the difference between them. Cotton had a 76 to lose by a stroke to the young South African. "You are a lucky young fellow," he told Locke, who filed away that patronising remark for future vengeance.

Locke was further nettled on the morning of their challenge match at Walton Heath the following week. Cotton arrived twenty minutes late on the tee, with no word of explanation or apology. Cotton, aided by his partner Reg Whitcombe, took a one-hole lead in the morning round and presented himself on the tee for the afternoon circuit 25 minutes late, again offering no apology. Locke decided that if time was such an insignificant factor in the match he might as well take plenty of it for himself. He surveyed each putt at inordinate length and without the benefit of help from his partner, Brews, went out in 30 to put the South Africans two up. Locke relished the reaction he detected in Cotton as putt after putt found its mark. Cotton began to play some wild shots while Locke continued his campaign of the most telling form of psychological warfare, holing putts. Locke was round in 63 and the South Africans were two holes up at the halfway stage.

The papers gave Locke a mauling for his funereal procession golf in the first two rounds. The South African was quite shaken by the severity of the criticism. He, Brews and Whitcombe arrived on the tee ten minutes early for the third round and found Cotton waiting for them. Cotton and Whitcombe buckled down to their task, played fine golf and took a one-hole lead into lunch. In the final round Locke went out in 32 to regain the lead for the South Africans. At the twelfth Cotton played the most celebrated golf shot of his career.

The hole measured 391 yards as played down the dog-legged fairway. Cotton was noted for his long (and straight) driving but he always gave the impression that he had twenty or thirty more yards in reserve for emergencies. And for two great champions to be trailing a couple of unknown whippersnappers from South Africa, with holes running out, this was an emergency. Cotton waved the crowds back and set himself to take the direct route, over a wilderness of scrub and trees to the unseen green. He put everything into his drive and the ball finished a yard short of the green, in the fringe. Even Locke, not Cotton's greatest fan at that time, was overcome by astonishment and admiration for the greatest drive he had ever seen. With the benefit of a brisk following wind, an absolute necessity before even contemplating such a do-or-die shot, Cotton carried that drive some 350 yards through the air. The inevitable birdie from such a killer blow squared the match and the English champions swept on to a 2 and 1 victory. Immediately afterwards Locke's backer sent Cotton a challenge for $1,000 to play Locke in a head-to-head match the following year. Cotton declined on the grounds that Locke was not a champion, nor even a member of the PGA.

Locke remedied both those eligibility requirements in due season, winning four Open championships, but he was never able to tempt Cotton into single-handed combat. They met again in another fourball match, in 1952 at Walton Heath again, with the Ulsterman Fred Daly as Cotton's partner and the mercurial Scot Eric Brown partnering Locke. This was a much more professional affair and the Cotton-Daly combination took the £750 prize by 8 and 7.

The pinnacle of Cotton's career as a match-player was probably when he won the 1932 British match-play championship, sponsored by the *News of the World*, by beating Alf Perry in the final. Bernard Darwin wrote of the last day's play:

It is difficult to restrain oneself about Cotton's golf in the final. My inclination is to say that I have never seen such golf played – no, not by Bobby Jones nor Sarazen nor the Triumvirate (Harry Vardon, James Braid and J. H. Taylor) nor anyone else. I will curb my enthusiasm, but I can safely say that I never saw better golf, for that would be impossible. Moor Park measures 6,500 yards and the ground was very wet. Cotton's score for 28 holes was nine under an average of fours. There really seems no more to be said. From tee to green I did not see him make one single shot with which any fault could be found. Twice he took three putts, but in each case his first putt was from the very edge of a big green, and, goodness knows, he made up for these two tiny slips by holing a cruel number of long ones. In fact, he putted, as he did everything else, quite magnificently. I am sure he has never been so good a golfer as he is today.

Another growth area during Cotton's career was the rise in public interest in international team matches. It remains an historical curiosity why this development was so slow. After all, the nationalistic element in challenge matches gave them an obvious added zest, as in the case of Taylor versus Kirkaldy. The first professional team match did not take place until 1913. It was an informal affair, arranged by the players themselves, and so strictly speaking not a truly representative contest, between the United States of America and France. It was played at Versailles and Arnaud Massy, Louis Tellier, Jean Gassiat and Pierre Lafitte beat Johnny McDermott, Mike Brady, Tom McNamara and Alex Smith. There was no opportunity for a return match because professional golf went into abeyance until another international encounter at Versailles five years later resulted in a treaty which brought peace to Europe for the next twenty years.

The golf editor of a New York newspaper, Jim Harnett, was responsible for setting in train the events which led to the establishment of the Ryder Cup matches. He solicited contributions from his readers to send a team of American professionals to challenge the British players. Emmett French was appointed captain and he selected the other members of the team: Walter

Hagen, Tommy Armour, Wild Bill Melhorn, Wilfred Reid, Jock Hutchison, Fred McLeod, Tom Kerrigan and Jim Hackney. That 1921 match was played at Gleneagles and resulted in such a humiliating defeat for the invaders that the American Ambassador departed the scene in a distinct huff. The only note of consolation for the Americans was that the visit enabled Jock Hutchison to return to his birthplace, St Andrews, and win the Open championship.

Walter Hagen, never a man to brood over reverses, remained enthusiastic about such matches and in 1926 he and his manager, Bob Harlow, organised another team. The match was played at Wentworth and again the Americans were overwhelmed, by 11 points to 1. Hagen's opponent in the singles was again George Duncan, who repeated his earlier victory, by 6 and 5. Then in the foursomes Hagen and Jim Barnes were turned over 9 and 8 by Duncan and Abe Mitchell. That was a fortuitous pairing because Mitchell had been appointed personal pro to Samuel Ryder, a wealthy seedsman from St Albans who had made a fortune from pioneering penny packets of seeds. Ryder took up golf on the advice of his doctor after suffering a nervous breakdown from overwork and, under Mitchell's guidance, became a useful six-handicapper with a reputation as an exceptional putter. He once single-putted all 18 greens in a competition at his home club of St Albans. Ryder was mayor of St Albans, a justice of the peace and a considerable Shakespeare scholar. But above all he was obsessive about golf.

Harlow and Ryder joined the foursome after the match for tea and all agreed that such matches were good for golf and international relations. Hagen pointed out that the Americans had made the trip twice and that transatlantic ships sailed in both directions. Duncan responded that either way they charged for the passage, in dollars or pounds. At this point Ryder made his first contribution to the discussions: "How much?" The upshot was that he agreed to provide a trophy and arranged for *Golf Illustrated* to open a subscription list to raise the £3,000 expenses for a British team to play in America in the first of a series of biennial matches. He would personally underwrite any shortfall. That was a good start although after that first subsidised year the PGA had problems in finding the cash for the overseas trips. Sir Stuart Pearson, a notable benefactor of professional golf, offered the PGA a million pounds to endow the matches some years later but his offer was declined.

The first match for Sam Ryder's gold chalice, surely the most beautiful trophy in sport, was played at Worcester, Massachusetts, in 1927 and the Americans won by a margin almost as embarrassingly wide as they had been beaten at Wentworth, 9½ to 2½. Two years later later Cotton was brought into the team. The match was played at Moortown and Cotton, after losing a tight match in partnership with Ernest Whitcombe in the foursomes against Walter Hagen and Johnny Golden, became the hero of the hour when he secured the winning point by beating Al Watrous 4 and 3 in the singles. That match was chiefly memorable, as far as he was concerned, for a stroke of outrageous luck when he holed out with his niblick from some bushes at the 18th to win a hole which had seemed irretrievably lost.

Cotton refused to play in the 1931 team which travelled to Scioto, Ohio, because he was in dispute with the PGA over its decision that all money won by players during the trip should be pooled. He covered the matches in his capacity as golf correspondent to the *News of the World*. The trophy was duly won back by the Americans. The Ryder Cup charter required team members to be native-born and residents and this rule had disqualified a number of players from the American pioneering team of 1921, including Armour, McLeod and Hutchison. Now it excluded Britain's strongest player for the 1933 match because Cotton by then was resident in Belgium as the professional at Royal Waterloo. He did not play again until 1937 at Southport and Ainsdale. He and Dai Rees were the only British winners in the singles and the Americans won by 8 points to 4, a result which was to be repeated with humiliating regularity in the years that followed.

Cotton was appointed captain for the first post-war team, to play at Portland, Oregon. With the war scarcely over and the PGA's coffers empty, it had seemed doubtful whether the British would be able to keep this engagement. The Canadian industrialist, Robert Hudson, came to the rescue and financed the trip. It was not the happiest of occasions. Cotton put the American backs up by complaining that the faces of their clubs had been roughened to impart extra backspin. The suspect clubs were changed and the Americans severely punished the visitors for their effrontery. Cotton suffered one of the heaviest defeats of his life in partnership with Arthur Lees, beaten 10 and 9 by Porky Oliver and Lew Worsham in the foursomes, then going down 5 and 4 to Sam Snead in the singles.

Ben Hogan, non-playing captain of that team following the road accident which almost took his life, had been stung by Cotton's effrontery in questioning the legality of the American clubs and two years later, when the Americans arrived at Ganton for the 1949 match, the first thing he did as captain was to object to the face markings of Dick Burton's clubs. It was agreed that the suspect clubs should be sent to an independent arbitrator, Bernard Darwin, the golf correspondent of *The Times* and a former chairman of the Rules of Golf Committee. The emissaries had to wait for some time because Darwin was in his bath when they arrived at his hotel. His verdict was summary: "Nothing a little filing won't put right." Hogan retired to his bed with the satisfaction of knowing that men were working through the night in the workshop at Ganton and that a score had been settled, if only partially. Cotton was not in the team that year so the culprit of Portland escaped Hogan's vengeance.

Cotton was non-playing captain for the next visit of the Americans, to Wentworth in 1953. His approach to the job was typically robust and controversial. He had the team accommodated in great comfort in the dormie house at Sunningdale and made sure that the food was of the very best, with plenty of steaks and fresh fruit in accordance with his own dietary laws. The controversial aspect of his captaincy was that he banned wives. His motive had nothing to do with the old boxing myth that sex sapped the stamina and made the legs go wobbly in the later rounds. Indeed, events were to suggest that celibacy, if anything, did that. He could only play eight men each day from his ten-man team and he did not want the wives around spreading dissension in the camp with their pillow talk criticising his selections.

There is no doubt that Cotton was an inspiration to his players, particularly in his thoroughness in organising practice sessions and trying different foursomes combinations. The only criticism of him from the players, and from a minority of them at that, was his insistence that they all had a rest after lunch. The first day's series of foursomes was a disaster, 3–1 to the United States. The newspapers ran lurid stories about Cotton castigating his men and criticised his pairings. Toots went round Wentworth tearing down the offensive newspaper bills advertising these scandals: "COTTON KICKS RYDER CUP MEN". The enterprising photographers put up fresh bills, took up points of vantage and had their cameras ready focused for the moment when Toots returned to rip them down again.

As the draw turned out, the British and Irish team's babes, Peter Alliss and Bernard Hunt, looked to have favourable chances, against Jim Turnesa and Dale Douglas, respectively. With Fred Daly, Eric Brown and Harry Weetman all winning their matches, the issue was delicately poised for a famous home victory. Alliss, one up with three to play, lost the 34th where he missed a two and a half-foot putt, drove out of bounds to lose the 35th and then fluffed a chip and missed a three-footer at the last which would have secured half a point. He was crucified by the press and press criticism of his play of those three holes soured his disposition for years and induced a neurosis about short putts which plagued him to the end of his playing career.

Then Hunt came to the last green where he needed to get down in two putts to beat Douglas and save the match. He took three putts. Instead of ending on the anticipated note of triumph, Cotton's association with the Ryder Cup finished in bitter anti-climax and recrimination. It is curious to reflect how reputations can be made and lost in golf by events outside one's control. If Hunt and Alliss had won their matches they would, obviously, have been hailed as heroes and, certainly in the case of Alliss, a formidable striker at this time, he might have gone on to become a great champion. But it is all too easy to imagine the odium which would have befallen Sam Snead in that case because his game had gone completely to pot towards the end of his single with Weetman. He drove into the trees at hole after hole and threw six holes in succession at the grateful Weetman.

Chapter 12

When the captain of the Professional Golfers' Association, Alf Padgham, arrived at Royal St George's golf club, Sandwich, to play a practice round before the 1934 Open championship he was told that he must change in the professional's shop. At this period the fee for a playing round with a professional was the same as the caddie's. It was partly this attitude towards golf professionals, reinforced by snide criticism from his contemporaries and the guttersnipe press, that had persuaded Cotton to work on the continent.

In Belgium he did not enjoy the regal treatment given by the Americans to their golfing heroes, such as Walter Hagen, but at least the members of the Royal Waterloo club were immune from the English disease of golf snobbery. They appreciated Cotton for what he was and happily paid the scale of fees which their 'prof' deemed appropriate for his expert services. In Britain Cotton was widely held to be arrogant, uppity and overly eager to feather his own nest. There was just enough truth in these charges to make them sting but in one important respect the half-truth represented a complete falsehood. Certainly Cotton made no bones about his own ambitions to make a fortune from golf. But he was absolutely genuine in his ambitions for the entire profession; he wanted every professional golfer to enjoy a higher social status and a much higher standard of reward.

Rather curiously as it may seem, the old champions, who might have been expected to be set in their traditional ways and content with their standing as popular servants, understood Cotton's objectives and supported him wholeheartedly. J. H. Taylor,

Harry Vardon, James Braid and Sandy Herd gave him every encouragement. And the very junior professionals were with him. Eddie Whitcombe, nephew of Reggie, the best of the three Whitcombe brothers, often played exhibition matches with Cotton who insisted that he conduct the business of negotiations. Cotton would negotiate a fee of some £50 for himself, adding that young Whitcombe's fee would be 18 guineas. Eddie Whitcombe recalled with gratitude: "In fact I would never have had the nerve to ask for as much as that; more like half."

It was against this background that Cotton and Toots arrived at Sandwich in his crimson Mercedes for the 1934 Open championship. He knew very well that he would never get anywhere in his campaign to break down the barriers of prejudice and snobbery in Britain unless he commanded the authority which is invested in the champion golfer. His example as an *émigré* club professional would carry no weight, especially as the forces of both masters and slaves were united in preserving the status quo.

There was therefore much more than self-interest behind Cotton's craving for success in the championship. His normal practice was to begin preparing for the Open the day after the conclusion of the previous championship and after eight attempts his obsession was becoming tainted with a tinge of desperation. He had twice scented victory, at Hoylake in 1930 when he injured his right wrist after a promising start, and the following year at Carnoustie where he was foiled by his own folly of listening to the advice of a magazine editor to play safe.

The portents for 1934 could hardly have been less auspicious. Cotton arrived at Sandwich with four sets of clubs and, in the words of his friend Henry Longhurst, could not hit his hat with any of them. The problem, as Cotton realised later, was that he was trying too hard. He was so consumed by the most important challenge of his life, and so desperate to succeed, that his mind was blocking his ability to swing properly. As every golfer of any attainment knows, it is impossible to play well if you are concentrating on the mechanics of what you are doing. Your instincts have been programmed to swing a golf club and they must be left free of interference to perform their task. The mind should be devoted to planning the shot, assessing distance, direction, shape and trajectory and visualising the ball's flight towards its target. All that information is absorbed by the subconscious which can safely be left to control the execution of the stroke.

This separation of the functions of the conscious and the unconscious mind can best be illustrated by analogy. Anyone can ride a bicycle along a winding path three feet wide. The eye sees the bends and passes that information to the subconscious which controls the physical functions of steering, balancing and pedalling without any conscious effort on the rider's part. He is free to employ his conscious mind on quite unrelated subjects, such as working out his income tax assessment. But elevate that three-foot path 200 feet into the air, across Niagara Falls, and the task of riding a bicycle becomes impossible. That was Cotton's problem at Sandwich. He had elevated the Open championship into a do-or-die ordeal and thereby sabotaged his instincts for hitting a golf ball.

After toiling all day on the practice ground in a state of mind fluctuating between panic and despair, he contemplated withdrawing from the championship since his quest was hopeless. Such a course of action, as he soon realised, would brand him as a quitter, provide ammunition for his critics and destroy his credibility. We may be sure that Toots expressed this view with some vehemence on the Saturday evening.

Cotton's fundamental golfing belief was that success could only be achieved through hard work. From the day he decided to become a professional golfer he had worked harder than any golfer before him at building his body into a golf machine and refining his technique. Even at the age of twenty-seven his body showed signs of the distortion which became so pronounced in later life. His right shoulder was dropped like a veteran fast bowler's, there was an incipient hunching of the shoulders from long hours of stooping over putts on the practice green. He had schooled himself to walk with a pigeon-toed gait because of his conviction that this style was more athletic and effective for golf than splayed feet. So his professionalism told him that he should spend the last day remaining before the qualifying competition working out his problems on the practice ground. His morale was at such a low ebb, however, that fatalism got the better of his judgment. Since he could not possibly win, and since winning was all that mattered to him, why torment himself further?

He decided to take the day off and not pick up a golf club again until he reported for the first qualifying round on Monday. In the event he did pick up a club on that Sunday but only in his capacity as caddie for Toots. That day off, and his abandonment of hope, for the championship, taught him a lesson which was to become one of his articles on golfing faith: the time to make swing changes is between tournaments; when you get to a tournament you must leave well alone and play with what you've got.

He was drawn to play very early on Monday morning at Royal St George's for the first qualifying round, with a marker. The timing was fortunate because there was no crowd to watch him. That eliminated one potential source of nervous tension. He had no expectations of his play. His attitude, as he wrote later, was "I might as well play now I am here, but I ought to quit." He went round in 66, without benefit of a single long putt, the most perfect round of golf he had ever played, reducing the twenty-year-old course record by two strokes. That round exorcised the demon and removed all the tension from the second qualifying round, to be played at Deal. It didn't really matter if he had an off day on the links of Royal Cinque Ports, with which he was not very familiar, because he was certain to qualify, as he did with a round of 75.

In the first round proper at Royal St George's Cotton was paired with Marcel Dallemagne, the French champion. As anyone can observe from inspecting the scoreboard at the tournament, it happens far too often for coincidence that all the players in one group have very good scores or, indeed, bad scores. There are many possible explanations. Certain golfers are popular as playing companions because the others benefit from watching the even tempo of their swings. The competitive element can come into it, a feeling that 'If he can do it, so can I'. The well-being which comes from agreeable companionship may well have an effect. It takes a very strong-willed golfer such as Jack Nicklaus to be able to shut out from his mind what is going on around him and to play his normal game without being influenced by his companions.

Cotton was certainly influenced, or possibly inspired is the better word, by Dallemagne's play. The Frenchman made a birdie at the first hole and Cotton almost drove the second green (the hole measured more than 350 yards) for his first birdie. Dallemagne sank a monstrous putt across the fifth green and Cotton matched him by chipping into the hole. Cotton had no success with his long putts but left every one close to the hole, to be out in 31. Dallemagne was 33.

There is no doubt that the solid foundation on which Cotton's game was based was his driving, as must be the case with every great champion. That statement is open to challenge from the example of such players as Billy Casper and Bobby Locke, both modest hitters from the tee. In both cases they preferred to sacrifice distance for accuracy and they were excellent drivers in the sense that they positioned the ball off the tee in the places they judged to give them the best lines of approach for the second shots. Cotton was so straight with the driver that Raymond Oppenheimer remarked that it was not possible to say whether his ball finished on the left or right side of the fairway. But he allied that accuracy with immense power, not always an advantage on links courses where the small ball, less responsive to fading and drawing, could run through winding fairways into the rough.

At the eleventh hole Cotton's power was his undoing. His drive found a bunker designed to catch an errant second shot and he dropped his only stroke to par for a solid round of 67. Dallemagne had a 71 to finish in a tie for third place with Densmore Shute of the United States and Alf Padgham, reckoned to be the best of the home-based rivals and destined to win the championship two years later.

Ridiculous as it may sound to the mathematically minded, numerical symbols in golf vary in value. In this case Cotton led by 3 strokes. But the man he led from was Fred Taggart of Wilmslow, no great shakes as a player as may be judged from the fact that he had taken 50 strokes from tee to green, as against the 36 allotted to first class players under the system of par rating. But Taggart had enjoyed 'one of those days' with the putter, requiring it only 20 times for his 70. It was quite out of the question that he might continue to match that rate of putting and he could be confidently discounted as a potential winner of the championship. (He went on to record scores of 76, 82, 77 for a share of 30th place.) Therefore Cotton's three-stroke lead was effectively and incontrovertibly four strokes. Furthermore, potentially the most dangerous threat to Cotton's ambitions, the American champion Gene Sarazen, had started with a 75.

Cotton's confidence was by now fully restored and he was at his peerless best for the second round. One stray shot at the eighth hole, into a bunker and a stroke lost against par, was the only blemish in a display of dominating power and flair. St George's is renowned for the treachery of its finish, through the gauntlet of rough and boundary fence at the 14th, the notorious Suez Canal hole; the daunting approach to the par-four 15th to a green of which it has been said that any golf course architect who designed it today would be locked up; the tee shot to the parsimonious and tightly booby-trapped green of the 16th; the tight drive up the undulating fairway of the 17th followed by an approach to a plateau and sharply tilting green; and finally the deceptive 18th, straightforward and innocuous enough to those who have never been humiliated by its subtle perils. Any golfer is happy to complete that stretch without losing a stroke or two to par.

Cotton, who had gone out in 33, played those holes in 4, 4, 3, 3, 3 to be round in 65. He had clipped a stroke off his own two-day-old course record, he had set a championship record which was to endure for more than fifty years with his two-round total of 132. And he had a seven-stroke lead, from Padgham. He knew that he had the championship in the bag if he could hang on.

The morning of the final day (36 holes at that time) was rainy and windy. Oddly enough, Cotton later described it as a lovely day at the seaside, bright sun and with a nice breeze. Actually, there was one rainstorm of such severity that the seventh green flooded and play was held up as the green staff cleared the water with squeegees. Cotton's 72 was the second best score of the round and left him with a lead of ten strokes, from the trick-shot specialist Joe Kirkwood.

Cotton was excited at the imminent prospect of the culmination of his dreams. He took a light lunch and made his way to the tee in good time, deflecting the congratulations of the thronging well-wishers with airy banalities about not counting chickens. It was entirely natural, of course, for the spectators to regard this final round as no more than a formality, almost a lap of honour, but Cotton well understood the danger in golf of anticipating triumphs or disasters. Yet his heart told him, as he wrote later: "It can't be otherwise, unless you are too stupid for it to be believable." When he arrived on the tee the starter told him that the time had been postponed by 15 minutes to enable the stewards to impose control on the excited throng. It was then that Cotton did something too stupid for it to be believable.

He went and sat by himself in a small tent by the first tee. His friends kept guard at the entrance to preserve his privacy. In the wisdom of hindsight he was to upbraid himself for not going away to hit some shots, to keep his muscles limber and his mind occupied. As it was his fertile imagination rehearsed all the possibilities for disaster. Does anxiety increase the acidity of the stomach in the way suggested for patent remedies against ulcers? Cotton's stomach was in a delicate state at the best of times and his doctor had put him on a strict diet. He developed fearful stomach cramp. He felt cold. When the starter called him he could hardly get to his feet. His friends were aghast at the pale, sweating apparition which emerged from the tent. He felt weak and sick. The effect of the stomach cramp was to restrict his follow-through. His opening drive was a low, raking hook into the rough from which he scrambled to a listless 5, one over par. At the second hole, which he had almost driven on the first day, he nobbled his drive and after three shots was still ten yards from the hole. He holed that putt and his putter saved his par figures at the next two holes. At the fifth he hooked into sand for a 6, missed the green at the Maiden to drop another stroke, three-putted the seventh and was still well short of the ninth green after three shots.

Most of his drives were low and hooked. J. H. Taylor was in despair and told those around him in the gallery: "He must get his left arm up." The pain of the stomach cramp prevented Cotton from making any movement approaching a full swing; it restricted him to a curtailed prod at the ball. He was out in 40, with the more difficult nine holes to come. He was headed for his fourth 5 in succession on the homeward run as he played the 13th. At that point he knew that Sid Brews had set a target score of 288 which meant that he had to score 83 to win. All the excited speculation about the margin of his victory and the records he would set had now been replaced by agonising over whether he could win at all. If he dropped four more strokes to par over the closing holes, easily enough done even by a golfer in good form, he would be the villain of the worst collapse in championship history. That would be the end of Henry Cotton.

He hit a fair drive down the 13th, followed by a long approach which finished near the green. He chipped to about ten feet. The putt went in for a birdie. "That seemed to cheer me up and I relaxed a little for the first time in two hours" he wrote in his usual laconic style in *This Game of Golf*. To the gallery that putt caused a complete transformation in Cotton's demeanour and in his play. From then he was back to the brilliant form of the first two rounds. He hit every green in regulation figures and narrowly missed his birdie putts on the 15th, 16th and 17th. His score of 79 gave him a total of 283, victory by five strokes.

For the first time in eleven years the trophy was to remain on the east side of the Atlantic. Cotton had no jacket with him and borrowed Henry Longhurst's camel-hair overcoat to receive the trophy. Would that modern winners of the championship were as punctilious about making themselves presentable for the presentation.

Harry Vardon, winner of the championship a record six times, was staying at the nearby Guildford hotel that week with his friend, Arthur Brown. For the first two rounds they had made their way slowly to the Maiden, the high dune which dominates the first nine holes, and selected a favourable vantage point to sit and watch the passing play. On the final day the ailing Vardon was too ill to follow this routine and remained in the hotel, following progress from reports brought back from the course by Brown. After the presentation, Cotton went to see his old friend, taking the ancient claret jug with him. They had never had a formal master and pupil relationship but Cotton acknowledged that he had learnt more about golf from Vardon than he had from his quests for enlightenment to America. They did not talk much on this occasion, the moment was too charged with emotion for words, but both shed tears.

Chapter 13

The Calvinistic streak which runs through the Scottish character is to be seen in every aspect of national life and never more evident than in the links of Carnoustie. There is no hint of frivolity about this bleak sweep of Tayside golf country; life is real and, above all, earnest. The course proclaims the harsh doctrine of Scottish golf: stray from the path of righteousness and you will suffer damnation. Golf has been a way of life in these parts for centuries. Hundreds of Carnoustie men emigrated to the Americas to teach the technique and ethics of the game, notably the Smith brothers, Alex, Willie and MacDonald, and Stewart Maiden who taught the game to Bobby Jones. Carnoustie men have won the championships of every state of the Union and the national championships of Britain, America, Canada, South Africa and Australia.

There are two courses, the Medal, or championship, course and the shorter Burnside. Both are public and half a dozen clubs in the town also play on the links. Allan Robertson, the first man to earn his living exclusively as a golf professional, laid out the original ten holes in 1839, formalising the haphazard system by which golfers made up holes on an *ad hoc* basis over the links which had been used for golf since the sixteenth century.

Old Tom Morris added eight holes in 1867, in compliance with the convention set by St Andrews that 18 holes constituted a round of golf. James Braid thoroughly revised the Medal course in 1926. His changes included the creation of the infamous Braid's bunker, slap in the middle of the second fairway which, when the course is in championship trim, leaves only seven yards of fairway on one side, five yards on the other. But if there is one person in whose belly the fire of God-fearing righteousness burns more fiercely than within a Scottish evangelist it is a Scottish chartered accountant. James Wright, chairman of the Carnoustie golf courses committee, improved and lengthened the course in readiness for the 1937 Open. He was mainly responsible for putting the sting, or at least increasing the venom, in the tail of the Medal course. With the serpentine Barry burn weaving its treacherous progress over those closing holes, Carnoustie has earned the reputation of having the toughest finish in the championship roster. Walter Hagen rated Carnoustie the finest course in Britain and among the best three in the world. Kind words come easily from a winner and his compliment was all the more sincere for having been made when Carnoustie held its first Open, in 1931, when Tommy Armour was the winner.

On that occasion Cotton made a fine start and led jointly with José Jurado after two rounds with a total of 147. His friend Eliot Cockel, publisher of *Golf Illustrated*, made an overnight journey from London to give Cotton the benefit of his tactical advice on how to win the Open. Cockel's plan was to avoid all risks in the third round and then to get the whip out for the sprint to the finishing line. To anyone who knew Cotton, it seems extraordinary that he took the slightest notice. But he did. He avoided all risks and compiled a meticulous 79 which effectively dished his chances of victory. Cotton finished in seventh place and reflected ruefully in his book *This Game of Golf*: "In golf there is no playing safe; the ball can still run against you wherever you hit it, as I realised, and there is no whip to take out, unless to beat yourself after the round for making a mess of things."

Another curiosity about Cotton's participation in that championship was that according to several books purporting to record the history of the championships he did not play. Doubtless perpetuating an original error, they relate how Cotton made a special visit to play Carnoustie in the spring of 1937 in preparation for the championship because he had never seen the course (on which he had finished seventh six years previously). Even Cotton's ghostly co-author repeated this oddity. Cotton did indeed visit Carnoustie in May 1937 but his purpose was to refresh his memory of the course and to familiarise himself with the revisions made by Wright.

In their usual expansive style the Cottons took over a boarding house for themselves and their friends for the two weeks of the 1937 Open. Among their guests was Leonard Crawley, one of the last of the great Corinthians and later to become golf correspondent of the *Daily Telegraph*. Crawley was an all-rounder in the mould of C. B. Fry, an outstanding golfer, a crack shot and a ferocious hitter of a cricket ball as captain of Essex. One Test player said of him: "The only way to bowl at Leonard is to let the ball go and duck for safety behind the umpire." In 1931 he had faced the exquisite dilemma of having to choose between playing for Great Britain and Ireland in the Walker Cup match or playing with Douglas Jardine's team on the famous bodyline Test series in Australia.

The entire American Ryder Cup team had entered for the Open, including the formidable trio of Byron Nelson, Gene Sarazen and Sam Snead. After practising with the Americans for a week and having watched them overwhelm the British for the first time on home soil, Crawley was insistent that no British player stood a chance in the Open. Burdened by this conviction, it was not too surprising that Crawley himself failed to qualify for the championship and immediately departed from the scene of an inevitable American victory.

This time Cotton resolutely ignored the wise golfing insights of a friend. For two rounds he played, as he put it, well enough but not outstandingly better than the others in the distinguished field for rounds of 74, 73. At this point he was equal sixth, behind Reg Whitcombe (142), Charles Whitcombe and Ed Dudley (144), Alf Padgham and Densmore Shute (146). Charles Lacey of the United States, brother of Arthur Lacey who captained the British and Irish Ryder cup team in 1951, was on 151 and well down the field, three strokes behind Arthur. Charles Lacey was to represent a considerable complication in the stirring events which were to follow on the final day.

Reg Whitcombe, the most successful of the three West Country brothers and destined to become champion the following year, was a very early starter in those days before the system of sending leaders out last. It was raining, and quite hard, but nothing like the deluge which was to develop as the day progressed. Taking advantage of the best of a vile day he went round in 74, to lead the field at the end of the third round by two strokes from his brother Charles, also 74. Cotton played a wonderfully controlled round of 72 to move into third place. Some idea of the conditions may be judged from the performances of the mighty Americans: Sam Snead 75, Densmore Shute 76, Ed Dudley 78, Horton Smith 79, Walter Hagen 80, Johnny Revolta 83.

Bernard Darwin described the conditions in his report for *Country Life*:

> The hollow in which the first green lies was on the last day getting more and more waterlogged as the day wore on, and the hole was being re-cut nearer and nearer to the slope on one side. There was an awful moment about lunchtime when a distinguished player refused to start on the justifiable ground that the first hole was unplayable. I remember Mr Norman Boase, the chairman of the championship committee, dashing through the rain to see if something could be done. Something was done, play went on, but all through the afternoon the authorities were on tenterhooks, and if anybody had lodged a formal appeal against the conditions I think it must have been upheld.

Charles Lacey hauled himself into contention with a 70, equalling the lowest score of the championship, and Byron Nelson had a 71 to move into the reckoning. They effectively represented the sole survivors of the vaunted American challenge and the huge crowd was in no way daunted by the worsening weather as violent rain squalls swept across the links. It was said that every umbrella and article of waterproof clothing available in the Carnoustie area had been purchased by spectators determined to witness another home victory. And it was quite evident that the man they wanted to win was Cotton, the hero who had ended an eleven-year era of American domination of the championship three years previously. This natural preference to see a hero endorse his status did not imply any indifference to the Whitcombes, for all three brothers were popular figures. But Cotton had done it before; he was the people's champion and had their trust.

This was probably the only championship in which Cotton had complete trust in himself. Toots was with him every inch of the way, of course, and as always he took comfort from her presence. But for once he did not need any external stimulus to bolster his courage and determination. He played, quite simply, the round of his life. With the ground staff making prodigious efforts to keep the greens in playable condition, and hampered by all the complications of wet grips and the chill from the downpour which penetrated to his skin, he made only one error in the first nine holes. At the seventh his drive was slightly pulled and that cost him a stroke against the par of the hole.

His putting on this occasion was magnificent. He was one of the few players to master the pace of his putts on those sodden greens and, thanks to single putts at the second and the par-five sixth, he was out in 35. That outward half has been described as the greatest nine holes of golf ever played, a performance to compare with anything produced by Bobby Jones, Harry Vardon, Ben Hogan or Jack Nicklaus. As to that, who can say? What can be said is that this nine holes was the crucial thrust in the winning of the championship. From now on he had to protect his advantage and husband the precious handful of strokes he had in reserve.

He played the next five holes in par and it is probably true to say that as he came through each of those holes unscathed he disposed of another potential contender. Some may argue that surely they disposed of themselves if they dropped strokes to par over that stretch. But in those horrendous conditions the dropping of a stroke to par cannot be harshly judged as a failure. He missed the green at the 15th hole with his approach and his chip was killed by water on the green, leaving him too far away to save par with a single putt.

Now for the toughest finish in British championship golf. Immaculate shots saw him safely through the 16th and 17th and he hit a good drive down the 525-yard 18th. His one concern now was the out-of-bounds fence down the left side of the fairway. His long drive had put him within striking distance of the green but it would take a big shot with its attendant risks from that boundary fence. His choices, then, were to lay up short of the burn which crosses the fairway in front of the green and pitch to the flag, the way the hole was designed to be played. Or he could go for the green.

Information from the course was nothing like so complete or reliable as it was to become, with computerised scores flashed instantaneously to every tee. Details of how other players were faring was passed by word of mouth and often inaccurate. It was understood by Toots, and relayed to Cotton, that a par five would be good enough for victory but he did not care to rely on hearsay. Besides, there were other players behind him who might change everything with a brilliant closing burst. In his confident mood he decided to go for a big one. He took his 2-iron and reduced the threat of the out-of-bounds by aiming as far right as he dared, wide of the green but to a target area from which he could chip sideways to the flagstick. His ball finished in the bunker guarding the right side of the green, level with the hole. Fearing that his broad-soled blaster might bounce on the hard, wet sand and make contact high on the ball, sending it across the green and out of bounds, he selected his thin-bladed niblick. His recovery shot from the bunker was by no means a classic example of sand play. The ball came out well enough but finished well short of the hole, as Cotton intended. By now he was assured that he had two putts to win and duly took them, for a round of 71 which maintained his progression of scoring a stroke lower in each succeeding round of the championship.

The partisan spectators, who had greatly warmed to Cotton since his return from self-imposed exile in Belgium to take up his appointment at Ashridge, went wild with delight, even though technically Cotton had not yet won. Mathematically Charles Lacey could still match or even beat Cotton's total of 290. But it would need him to clip a stroke off the course record of 70, which he had equalled in the third round, and in these dreadful conditions that faintest of possibilities disappeared over the closing holes. He returned a 72 for third place behind Reg Whitcombe. Cotton did not linger at Carnoustie to celebrate his triumph. He and Toots drove home through the night but not before he had savoured a telegram of fulsome congratulations from a humbled Leonard Crawley.

Chapter 14

*T*he long illness which resulted in Cotton being invalided out of the RAF, followed by a serious stomach operation and his doctors' decree that he must not so much as touch a golf club for a year, was a dispiriting period. Cotton was at an age when golfers experience intimations of their sporting mortality and he was frustrated that the war had robbed him of the opportunity to ratify in the record books his status as the best player of his era.

He and the American amateur, Frank Stranaham, were pioneers in that they were the only golfers of international stature who could be described as athletes in the common sense of the term. Cotton had deliberately and methodically built his body into a golfing machine although, ironically, in the process he had severely damaged his digestive system. That knowledge had turned him into a fanatical food faddist and it was quite natural that he blamed Britain's post-war diet for his failure to win the 1947 Open championship at Hoylake.

His old skills were unimpaired, as witness his opening 69 which led the championship. But he did not have the stamina for four gruelling rounds of championship golf and tailed away. He resolved that he must train even harder and to do this he must go abroad where he could get proper food. By 'proper' food he meant all the things which were still restricted in Britain by rationing: sugar, meat, cheese, eggs, bacon, fats and milk. The weekly ration of these commodities was no more than a healthy trencherman would routinely consume at a sitting in the United States. Ed Lowery, famous as the ragamuffin caddie whose immortal exhortation "Just keep your eye on the ball, Francis" had encouraged Francis Ouimet to victory over the mighty Harry Vardon and Ted Ray in the 1913 US Open, and now a prosperous businessman, was particularly supportive in Cotton's wish to regain his strength in America.

To later generations who have been hounded into phobic trepidation by fashionable nutritionists warning of the dangerous, even fatal, potential of those rationed comestibles, Cotton's decision may appear unwise. The wartime diet, predominantly fresh vegetables, pulses and wholemeal bread, is nowadays extolled as the ideal regimen for long life, health and happiness, although we did not appreciate it at the time, even if the Ministry of Food did. Since we had never heard of listeria, cholesterol and salmonella, we pined for luscious steaks and cream cakes. Cotton's faith in 'proper' food may have been a form of self-deception, or possibly the trendy dietary theorists of today are practising a form of mass deception, but at all events Cotton returned to Britain fitter and stronger and more determined than ever to do well in what he knew must be one of his last realistic challenges for the premier prize in golf.

There may have been another, even more important, bonus from that trip to America in the spring of 1948. Starting with Cotton, all the great champions of the modern era, with the possible exception of Johnny Miller and Tony Lema, have been obsessive about preparing for the major championships. They become almost neurotic, practising certain shots they feel will be needed for the championship course, fiddling with their clubs, planning in minute detail what they will wear (often on the basis of their 'lucky' colours), reconnoitring and measuring a course with which they are already intimately familiar and even going down to such esoteric detail, as Bob Charles was apt to do, as asking other people to unscrew the tops off sauce bottles to eliminate the million to one chance of cutting their hands.

They know well enough that most of this preparation is of no practical value, and might even be self-defeating in making them over-anxious, but so long as there is the remotest possibility that something might help they will do it. They then enjoy the reassurance that they have done everything possible to give them the best chance of winning. That reassurance translates into the most potent weapon in a golfer's armoury, confidence, and Cotton returned to Britain with his confidence fully restored and ready for action.

Cotton had a reputation as a fast starter whose main problem was to maintain his early advantage over the long haul of four rounds. A detailed study of his scoring record adds little statistical weight to that theory although he himself conceded that there might be something in it because of his excitable nature. In the later stages of a championship the ghosts of past failures returned to taunt him and the nervous energy needed to maintain his composure was certainly draining. In any case his temperament demanded that he put more into his golf than most of the competitors and consequently the game took more out of him. The manner of his first championship victory at Sandwich undoubtedly served to put an undue emphasis on his questionable staying power in the public mind.

At Muirfield there was therefore a certain reserve attached to the rejoicing over his first round 71, a fast enough start to leave him right up among the leaders. The next day King George VI arrived to watch play and wished good luck to the man with whom he had enjoyed many rounds. They shook hands and Cotton was inspired to produce a golfing dish fit to set before a king. An ill-judged chip from the side of the third green, needing two putts to complete the hole, was the only blemish in an opening half of 33 which ended with the flourish of an eagle on the long ninth. With the king applauding every stroke, Cotton continued to produce golf of exhibition quality for a course record 66 which left the field floundering in his wake. His close friend Percy Boomer remarked: "Only one man can beat Henry and that's Henry himself." Cotton's putting, always his Achilles' heel, betrayed him for a third round 75 and Alf Padgham moved up within striking range, two strokes behind after three solid rounds.

This turn of events did not dent Cotton's confidence. Although he practised his putting assiduously and analysed the mechanics of the stroke, he retained a measure of the superstitious attitude of the early professionals that good putting was held in the gift of mysterious forces beyond the control of man. He was fatalistic about the afternoon, trusting that his putting touch would be restored to him but so secure in the superiority of his long game that he was sure he could prevail even without the benefit of exceptional putting.

Cotton was fond of remarking: "One day you've got it and the next day it's gone." That is a common enough experience among

all golfers but at least the professionals who followed, most notably Bobby Locke, looked for rational explanations for this mystery and in his case found some of them. It was Padgham's turn to
lose his putting stroke in the final round. He took 77 and Cotton's
72 gave him victory by five strokes.

The margin of his win and the fact that there was only a token
representation of American stars in the field has tended to down-
grade Muirfield as the least of Cotton's championships. It is true
that he was not put to the test of intense competition but in some
respects it was his greatest triumph. To pick up his career after
the four-year wartime lacuna and restore his game in the face of
serious problems with his health and then win the championship
at the age of 41, playing one of the historic rounds in the annals of
golf, was a considerable achievement. It required a supreme effort on his part and he knew immediately the championship was
over that it would be his last.

He would go on playing but he never deceived himself that he
might have another championship in him. He must seek new
challenges and satisfactions from the game. Having faced the
painful truth of his declining powers, most evident in a collapse of
his always vulnerable touch with shot putts, Cotton was interested
to discover whether his predecessors had similarly recognised the
point in their careers when they realised that they had started to
descend the far side of the infamous sporting hill.

Some reacted vigorously to such a question and Cotton's impish
sense of fun prompted him to try the question on younger
players. Bernard Gallacher, for instance, was quite taken aback
when Cotton asked him: "Can you pinpoint the exact moment
when you realised you were finished?" It is true that by this time
Gallacher had cut down on his tournament programme and had
taken an appointment as professional to the Wentworth club but
he was still in his mid-thirties and by no means saw himself as a
spent force. Indeed, he was to win again, possibly spurred on to
emphasise his indignant denial. In truth, Gallacher's indignation
was momentary because he had been around Cotton long enough
to appreciate his penchant for lobbing conversational hand
grenades.

Chapter 15

*C*otton's tall and slim physique was deceptive. He habitually wore long-sleeved shirts and tailored slacks for golf and his outfits were very carefully chosen, both for understated elegance and to disguise the disproportionate development of his golfing muscles. Reg Whitcombe described his forearms as resembling other men's calves and on the occasions when Cotton wore plus-fours it was plain to see that his calves were almost heifers. He had deliberately structured himself with selective body-building exercises into his ideal of a golfing machine, based on his highly personal and controversial concept of golf as a game to be played mainly with the hands.

To over-simplify a highly complex subject, the received wisdom of golf theory was, and largely remains, that the club-head is accelerated by a rotation of the body multiplied by a downward pull of the arms to a point where centrifugal force takes over and carries the club-head through the impact zone, with the wrists acting purely as free-swinging hinges. The ball is almost incidental; it simply happens to be located on the path of the swinging club-head at the point where the speed is at its maximum. In other words, the golf swing was a flail action in which the only function of the hands was to hold on to the grip.

From his earliest days as a teenager Cotton became convinced that the hands had a much more vital contribution to make. He became obsessive about building up the strength of his hands and spent hours scything thick rough with a club and squeezing squash balls. And, while he assiduously watched and questioned great players and experimented with their methods, he never wavered in his belief that the hands held the key to golf.

His schoolboy swing produced a natural fade and on his first visit to the United States he was persuaded, by the counsel of Sam Snead and others, that he would have to master the technique of drawing the ball from right to left if he was ever to command enough length to compete at the highest level. In the classical, flail swing, the hands naturally roll anticlockwise through the impact zone. But this necessarily has to be a left-sided action, causing conflict within pupils who find it difficult to understand (and even more difficult to obey) exhortations not to let their right hands dominate the action. Why not? Their main strength lies in their right hand and yet they are not to use it.

For a while Cotton was attracted by the prevailing view that there must be a perfect golf swing, a method which optimised all the potential of the body's major muscles to deliver the maximum power at impact. This would be the standard swing which every-one should employ. He studied the actions of all the great players, experimented with their styles and copied elements which he felt he should incorporate into his own game. This search for golf's holy grail proved fruitless, as it has for many others, and he wrote that it was not until he decided that he could not play like the golfers he had tried to copy that he made much progress. He became persuaded by the evidence of watching the individual methods of the great masters of the game that a universal swing could not and should not be imposed on all golfers, regardless of their shape and size. The bespoke swing, incorporating certain fundamentals but tailored for each individual, must be the way.

Cotton set about cutting out the pattern for his own golf and the first requirement he demanded was that the right hand should not only make its due contribution but that it should be the very key to his golf. He liked to illustrate his point by recounting the story of a Frenchman who came to see him at Penina in a state of despair. This man had been receiving regular lessons from a French pro for six months and in all that time he had not been allowed to hit a ball. Monsieur le Prof had apparently selected this pupil as a guinea pig for an experiment in golf instruction, based on the theory that pupils became hypnotised by the sight of the ball and their attempts to hit it out of sight militated against the acquisition of a sound swing. The imagination falters at the thought of a man enduring six months of such self-denial but apparently this pupil did indeed devote six months to swinging a club without a ball, under the guidance of the pro. He perfected the motion of the swing through long hours of practice in front of a mirror at his home in the evenings. When the great day arrived and the pro deemed him ready to hit a ball the man felt certain, as the pro had assured him, that his patience and self-discipline would be richly rewarded; he would play like Ben Hogan right from the start. In the event he popped the ball along the ground about fifty yards and fled in outrage from his treacherous mentor.

Cotton confirmed that this golfer did indeed have a beautifully grooved, classic swing. The problem was that he had not learnt how to give the ball a hit. His hands had not been schooled to absorb the shock of an eight-ounce club-head travelling at 100 miles an hour and generating an impact value of a ton and a quarter. Fortunately, a cure was at hand from an exercise of Cotton's devising. He took the man to the practice ground and led him to a worn car tyre lying on the ground. "Forget all about golf technique," he commanded, "just hit that tyre as hard as you can with your seven-iron." The pupil took a slightly apprehensive swipe at the tyre. "Harder!" said Cotton, "Sting it! Make it jump from the fury of your blow." Reassured that the club did not break under such rough treatment the man began to belabour the tyre with a will. "Put more venom into it!" said Cotton. Satisfied at last that his pupil was operating at full power, Cotton dropped a ball alongside the tyre and said: "Now I want you to give the tyre as hard a whack as you can summon and then step back and repeat the action on the ball." The Frenchman did as he was bid and gazed in amazement at the sight of the ball soaring high into the distance. It was a miracle. In five minutes Cotton had given him what his pro back home had failed to achieve in six months, not quite a Hogan swing, perhaps, but palpably an effective golf shot.

It was sometimes said of Cotton's miracle cures that they did not last. Pupils would return home and find that the magic had worn off. Some telephoned him to complain about their relapses. Cotton's bantering response was invariably a counter-attack: "You have neglected the most important thing I told you – ten minutes of tyre drill every day. You can't play golf without strong, educated hands." So what was this vital tyre drill?

The equipment is cheap and simple: a cane, an old club and an even older tyre, preferably bald. The first point to bear in mind is that it is vital to work up gradually to the full routine since overdoing it on the first day can cause muscle strain and ruin everything. But within the span of one week, the usual length of stay for pupils under Cotton's tutelage at Penina, a graduated series of daily sessions on the tyre can produce astonishing improvements on the golf course. Lay the tyre down flat, preferably against a wall or a tree because once you get into the swing of things the tyre will jump about and it is a bore having to keep dragging it back into position. If you are doing the drill indoors do, please, first ensure that there is plenty of room to make a full swing without shattering a Ming vase or slashing the Rembrandt on the backswing. Take the stick in the left hand and beat out a tattoo of twenty-five backhanded taps against the side of the tyre, as fast as you can and taking the stick back only about a foot. Your instinct will instruct you to perform this exercise with a series of wristy flicks. Wrong! To get the benefit of this exercise you must keep the wrist rigid so that the stick is an extension of the arm. You should feel that you are tapping the tyre with the back of the left hand, holding the stick with the thumb on top and gripping it mainly with the pinkie and ringfinger. It will feel awkward and clumsy and that is a good sign because it demonstrates a vast potential for improvement in your golf. Most people believe that bad golf is caused by the right hand dominating the action. That is nonsense, as Cotton continually reiterated. The left hand is much more likely to be the culprit. Once you have that left hand under control with a correct grip and doing its job properly then you can safely let fly with all the power you can muster in the right hand. Twenty-five brisk taps is enough to start with and by now, if you have put enough effort into it, you should feel the first twinges in your complaining arm muscles. Without regripping the stick, lean across to the other side of the tyre and beat out twenty-five forehand taps as if slapping the tyre with the palm of your hand. Switch the stick to the right hand and repeat both exercises, employing a similar grip.

The next exercise is a larger version of the first. This time take the stick back about waist high and cane the tyre, exerting real force and venom. Do it as fast as possible and make the stick swish and whistle as it cuts through the air. When doing these exercises you should stand tall, with a straight back, and feet slightly apart as if addressing a golf ball. On the first day, if you have applied yourself to the task with uninhibited gusto, you should now be almost fit to drop. Grit the teeth and proceed to stage three. Take the club and hold it with both hands in a proper golf grip. Whether you prefer the overlap, interlock or two-handed grip, the essentials are that the third knuckle of both hands should be discreetly screened from your view as you look down at your hands. The left thumb should be on top of the shaft, the right thumb lying across the shaft. Taking the club back about waist high, belt the tyre as hard as you can. Forget about golfing style, apart from maintaining your proper grip, and simply concentrate on beating the tyre to death. Make it jump with the fury of your blows, using every atom of strength in your body. Twenty-five belts delivered as fast as you can is enough for a start. Don't forget to follow with a similar number of equally energetic backhanders. Finally, repeat the exercise using a full swing, twenty-five lusty hits. By now you should be as limp as a rag doll. And if next morning you feel that your upper body is being crushed in some fiendish, medieval torture device then you may be reassured that the exercises are doing you good. Repeat the routines morning and night until they become child's play. Then increase the dose, working up to fifty hits a session, then 100. For really advanced masochism once you have worked up to the full 100 stage, you can progressively add weight to the club by winding lengths of lead wire around the hosel and you can introduce the ultimate refinement of doing the club exercises one-handed.

Cotton and his tyre became famous throughout the community of golf. Portly American businessmen made pilgrimages to Penina, their heads full of theory about straight left arms, dominant left sides, leg action and finger pressure. They were, almost literally, putty in Cotton's hands. He enslaved them with his charm and wit. Cotton and the donkey-caddie, Pacifico, were an irresistible double act on the course and the magical transformations on the tyre, with the pupils suddenly hitting real golf shots for the first time in their lives, completed the conquest.

Cotton, ever with an eye for the main chance, duly capitalised on the euphoria he created. One of his ploys when playing a round with a visitor who had duly fallen under his spell was to observe the major fault in a player's technique. Then, after the man had made a particularly embarrassing hash of a drive, Cotton would say: "Let me have a look at your driver. Yes, just as I thought; the weight distribution in the head is all wrong for you. Here, give my driver a try. Now, when you swing, this is what I want you to do . . . " Armed with a tip that put his swing right, the man naturally hit a good shot. Amazing! Cotton would let the man finish the round with the wonder driver but he would not present it to him right away. The impression had to be created of soul searching before the making of a supreme sacrifice. But that evening, on returning to his room after dinner, the visitor would find the driver with a note saying something like: "Your need is greater than mine, old boy." And when the hotel bill was rendered the purchase of one driver would be itemised, at a greatly enhanced price. A contemporary of Cotton's, Maurice Bowyer, a noted clubmaker who made clubs for Bobby Jones in his youth when he served as an assistant to Jack White at Sunningdale, had a golf equipment company, Castle Golf. Bowyer was a great innovator and one of his inventions was a two-piece shaft. It was a good enough shaft but it never caught on commercially. Quite a few drivers fitted with that two-piece shaft were 'bought' by visitors to Penina after playing with Cotton. Nobody ever complained about the exorbitant price; most likely nobody even considered the price to be exorbitant. In any case the driver plus the value of the lesson constituted a bargain. And, ironically, those drivers are surely worth more today as collectors' items than the visitors paid for them.

Oddly enough, Cotton persisted in his search for the perfect putting method and the physical problems which plagued him throughout his career were partly the result of his attempt to make himself into his idea of a putting machine. He had a vision of how the body could be conditioned into becoming a mechanically consistent striker of putts and he practised so hard and so long in pursuit of this unattainable goal that on many occasions he had to be physically picked up and carried off the practice green because his body had become locked in the shape of a question mark. As a result he was an inconsistent putter, never better than adequate, and his record was undoubtedly blemished because his putting did not match the standard of the rest of his game.

Once he decided that he must find the best way for Henry Cotton to play golf he based his experiments on his conviction that the hands must be the paramount source of power and control. He always talked of hands, and squeezed squash balls or spring-steel exercisers until he was well into his seventies, but, of course, the real sources of his strength were the wrists and forearms.

To a golfer's eye, Cotton's style was both beautiful and slightly mysterious. He would take the club in what can only be called a caress, holding it so lightly that you wondered whether it might slip from his fingers at any moment. The act of grounding the club-head behind the ball was ritualistic, almost reverential in the care and precision of the operation. The gigantic feet were plonked solidly into position, with the toes pointing straight ahead. Then one stare of his aquiline eyes at the target would complete the preliminaries.

The delicacy of touch on the club was emphasised as he turned away because as his hands moved back the club-head remained at rest momentarily. He made a full shoulder turn, with the hips opening about 45 degrees and, like all good players, by the time the club reached its position at the top, a markedly short back-swing with the club-face in an open position, the lower body had already started to recoil. The downswing was so leisured that the onlooker wondered how on earth he could generate enough club-head speed to hit the ball any distance at all. The human eye could not follow the speed of the action as those mighty forearms whipped the club through the impact zone and so it seemed that it had not happened. The only image on the retina was of Cotton standing perfectly still, both feet solidly flat on the ground, his head immovable, looking at the spot from which his divot had been displaced. His extended right arm, with the back of the hand pointing at the sky, having rolled over the left, was waist high on the follow through before there was the slightest movement of the head to follow the progress of the ball.

The other characteristic Cotton action which was clearly dis-cernible was the snapping straight of the left leg to brace his body against the shock of impact. But here was the mystery. How could such a languid movement generate the sound of a whip-crack as the club met the ball? And what strange force was propelling the ball such an inordinate distance on a bee-line towards the target? The answer, of course, was that the whip-crack was produced by the unseen whip-lash of those forearms. The quickness of the hands did indeed deceive the eye. Only a player of prodigious strength and immaculate timing could play golf like Henry Cotton.

He did try to get his pupils to employ the same technique, however, despite the inadequacy of their physical capacity. One of his drills was to get a pupil to set up aiming right of the practice green. Now he would say: "I am a Japanese prison guard. You will hit your shot on that line right of the green but unless the ball finishes left of the flag I shall shoot you in the back of the neck."

That exercise is getting slightly ahead of the story because first the pupil had to undergo the ordeal of the hands message. He liked to start by asking the pupil to hit half a dozen shots one-handed, first with the right, then with the left. The effect of this introduction was twofold. First, the pupil would suffer acute embarrassment at his pathetic attempts at one-handed golf, along with a considerable amount of discomfort; second, it established in the clearest possible way who was the master and who the helpless inadequate, rising young pro or Walker Cup player though he might be.

Cotton would then reinforce this painful lesson by picking up a fairway wood and lashing 200-yarders (about 85 per cent of his normal full shot) with his left hand before switching the club to his right and belting more balls to join the tight cluster at the far end of the practice ground.

Cotton would next offer the pupil some faint hope of regaining a shred of self-esteem by announcing that they could move on to hitting two-handed shots with the normal grip. Now, thought the hotshot golfers, was their chance to show the Maestro that they were not complete mugs. Cotton would arrange a dozen balls in a row and ask the pupil to hit one after another without reforming his grip on the club. This may not sound too difficult, but just try it. After two or three shots, sometimes after the first one, the club would twist in the pupil's grip, rendering further progress hope-less. This was Cotton's chance to rub home the message of the hands. With his row of balls he would hit one perfect shot after another, shuffling along the line and swinging in one recipro-cating movement. After this demonstration the chastened pupil would be only too willing, and anxious, to absorb what Cotton had to say about the place of the hands in the golf swing.

One of the great pleasures in life for a student of golf was to sit by the practice ground of Penina and watch Cotton's technique with a pupil who came to him with the attitude: "I'm a scratch player and there's nothing much you can tell me about how to play this game." Cotton relished such a challenge, particularly if it came from an arrogant American. "Just hit a few shots for me," he would say, in a tone inviting the pupil to show off. Cotton was extravagant in his praise and encouragement, urging the player to demonstrate his skill with different clubs. When he judged that the pupil was becoming arm weary, as any golfer must after hitting twenty or so shots without a break, Cotton would remark innocently: "You could hit the ball twenty yards farther if you used your hands better." Then he would put the pupil through the one-handed and hitting-without-regripping routine and quietly savour the onset of embarrassment and humility.

Cotton well understood the attitude which many pupils have towards teachers. "It is all very well for him; he's been at it full time all his life and it's second nature to him now. He doesn't know how I feel, or understand about my bad back, or realise how difficult this damn game is for somebody who has to sit in an office five days a week. I hope he doesn't try to make me use that stupid Vardon grip because unless I hold the damn club like a baseball bat I can't hit the ball out of my own shadow." Cotton understood all too well. He had a remarkable facility for picking out a golfer's main fault and correcting it with a simple exercise or instruction. The result was an instant and dramatic improvement in the pupil's striking and the conversion of a sceptic into an adoring disciple.

Naturally, the technique varied with each pupil and, apart from his emphasis on the hands, he made no attempt to impose a preconceived Cotton style. Each pupil was given a bespoke golf swing according to his or her size, shape and strength, a method which would enable him to get the most from his potential.

As he taught he expounded his philosophy of golf. He himself wrote several books on golf technique, and innumerable newspaper articles, so it is impossible to do full justice to the range of his ideas in a compressed version. But there is a common thread running through all his instructional writing and an attempt may perhaps be made to distil the essence of it.

The golfer who attempts to play by positional changes of the body, with passive hands, condemns himself to loss of control and almost certain back trouble in the long run. The hands hold the club and they must take priority in the swing, both to control the club-head and to supply its energy. The rest of the body moves to accommodate the paramount action of the arms, wrists and hands. Your swing can only be as effective as your ability to hang on to the club at impact and your hands can never be too strong. Exercise them as much and as often as you can.

The correct tension of the fingers throughout the swing is loose at first, tightening at impact and then relaxing again. This sequence will occur

*without conscious thought on your part provided you start the action with a
light grip on the club. How light is light? Exert just enough pressure with
the fingers to prevent the club from turning during the stroke.*

*The hands must move faster than the rotation of the body through the
impact zone, hitting past the body rather than with it. To achieve this
acceleration the right hand rolls over at impact and hits past the left hand.
Remember, this is a rolling action, not a cupping of the left wrist combined
with a forward bend of the right wrist, not a hinging action but a natural
twisting movement.*

*The right hand guides the shot and finds the ball. If you grip the club
with the palms in the same plane as the club-face you will automatically
square the club-face at impact, as instinctively as you would deliver a blow
absolutely flush when slapping someone's face. Feel that you are making a
definite 'hit' with the hands. Slicing is mostly caused by failing to sling the
club-head through the ball with the right hand. If you have the club-face
closed at the address position it is impossible to apply proper hand action.*

Hands, always the hands. The stronger they are the better you
can play. Most social golfers will despair at the message because
they simply do not have the time or opportunity to train their
hands to the degree necessary for playing the Cotton way. The
tyre drill may not take all that much time but even that is an
inconvenience and a chore which only the most enthusiastic
golfers will willingly undergo every day. Well, there is a simpler
method of strengthening the hands which can be done more or
less anywhere and at any time. Raise the arms in the surrender
position and then clench and unclench the hands as hard and as
fast as you can until you feel that your forearms are about to
explode. Anyone can do that while putting on a shirt and this
daily exercise will quickly condition the hands and forearms for
better golf the Henry Cotton way.

For the last twenty years of his life Cotton's main interest was
helping young professionals. By his own efforts he had turned
professional golf into a respected and lucrative career and revital-
ised the standing of British pro golf. He wanted the standards he
had set to be maintained and he enjoyed passing on the lessons he
had learnt by painful trial and error. For the groups of young
professionals who visited him at Penina, a week in Cotton's
company was a crash course in how to become a champion, a
combination of finishing school with heavy emphasis on personal
appearance, deportment and making a point of sending 'thank

you' letters to everyone who gave any kind of help, and a rigorous physical training and golf improvement course. He never made any charge for his instruction to young pros; fat fees were due only from 'civilians'.

At one session on the practice ground *Golf World* magazine tape-recorded Cotton's remarks as his pupils took a break from their labours.

"You hook with your left hand and slice with the right. Hit shots one-handed if you want to prove it. Most people think it's the other way round.

"A left-hand glove helps you to hold on, but it has to fit tight. It provides a consistent surface between the hand and the club, particularly on a hot day. Remember, the left hand, the top hand, is vital. All the pull is on it. If it is firm the right hand can float.

"If you are having trouble holding on, try a double-handed grip.

"Be honest with yourselves. You may be able to kid the rest of the world but not yourselves. If the club slips, admit it and work on it, because it's wrong. The left hand is the one that matters. A few good players let the club slide in the right hand deliberately, perhaps because of a stiff right wrist. But the left hand never lets go. If it does the contact is never solid. The ball is struck a glancing blow. You say 'I hit behind it, I dropped my shoulder, my hips turned too much.' Be honest. The club flew out of your hands.

"Look at this chap. Hopeless. He lets go every time. If he tries to hold on he chokes himself. If I were him I wouldn't bother to play golf until I had strengthened my hands. Six weeks' work on his hands and you wouldn't recognise him.

"You can't be too strong for golf. The idea is to over-train yourself, so that hitting a golf ball is as easy as hitting a ping-pong ball.

"Thousands of people have good swings but they are not strong enough to stand up to the shock of the club hitting the ball. Their hands and arms quit at impact because they aren't strong enough.

"You all let go of the club at impact. Has anyone ever told you that before? You've looked at your legs, your pivot, at this and that bit. Don't bother. The real trouble is in your hands. You can all swing well. You can hit the ball. But the shot to the right, then one to the left, one high, one low – it's in the hands. They are letting go, quitting. They're not strong enough.

"Exercise. Over-train yourselves. Squeeze grips in your fingers and work your wrists at the same time. Keep a pair of grips in your pockets and do it all the time. Hit the ball one-handed until you can't, then change to the other hand and give that a thrashing, then go back to the other hand. Put balls down all over the place and walk about and hit them. Make your hands find the ball. Tee up a dozen balls and hit them non-stop.

"Whatever method you want to play remember that the hands must be strong. It may not matter if you are shut or open at the top so long as your hands will bring the club-face square at impact. This is the 'secret' of golf.

"Betting is the way to toughen your game. Always bet on everything, even if it is only a shilling.

"Do press-ups on your finger tips. Can you do them? Let's see. No, not really. Little Gary Player came to me six years ago (1956) and asked me what he had to do to become a champion. I told him that he must above all work to make himself strong and fit. Look at him now, top money winner in America. And he can do 60 press-ups on his fingers, back straight as a ramrod – with a suitcase on his back to make it more difficult.

"It is harder for me to hit balls with my right hand alone than my left. At one time I could hit a four-iron 160 yards with my left hand. But the right hand must be trained too. It controls and directs the face of the club.

"In the grip the Vs (the creases between the thumbs and forefingers) of the hands must never oppose. If they do the hands will tend to slide on one another. The palms must be square to each other. In my own grip I like to keep the palms square to the club-face, too.

"There are very few people in the world whose hands are good enough to hang on to the golf club when they are swinging flat out. The speed and the shock of impact are tremendous. That's why many of the moderns 'push' the ball. They are choking up on the shots, hitting at less than full power, in order to keep control.

"Only a very few can make the grade as top tournament players. If you don't make the grade, don't be disheartened. There's a wonderful life for you as a club professional.

"The fact that you are assistants and that you have to be in the shop while your boss plays and practises and teaches shouldn't stop you from being good. What's wrong with getting out there at seven in the morning? And you don't always have to hit balls to train yourselves. Walk or cycle a little more and drive a little less. When you are sand-papering a wood or cleaning shoes do it much harder than necessary. Make yourself strong. Over-train yourself.

"To be good you must put the game of golf before everything else, before a wife and family, before cigarettes and alcohol, before everything. You have to be both selfish and self-sacrificing.

"Above all, be honest with yourselves. Don't kid yourselves that you are better than you are. Get a notebook and write down an honest analysis of every shot you hit, every round you play. Get a true picture of your ability. And don't go to tournaments until you are satisfied that you are good enough. To go simply in hope is a waste of time and money."

Afterword

*B*iographies should not be written by friends. That cardinal rule of publishing had to go by the board in the case of Henry Cotton. The biographer had to be someone in golf in order to interpret the technicalities of the game but where could you find a golfing writer who could review his character and career dispassionately? Doubtless there are young writers who never met him but that is not to say they are emotionally untouched by him. He aroused strong feelings of like or dislike, sometimes both simultaneously, and his death is too recent to have neutralised this capacity for engaging the emotions.

My association with Henry began in the sixties as a disciple anxious to pick his brains. Many golfers have devoted their lives to achieving complete control over the golf ball but only a handful of them have, in the words of Tom Watson, actually smelt and briefly touched that mastery. Henry was one of them in the years leading up to the second world war, as Laddie Lucas relates in his expert introduction to this book, and I wanted to learn everything I could about the legendary golfing holy grail which he had actually held in his hands. That phrase held the answer, for Henry insisted that anyone who wished to master golf must be prepared to devote as much time and energy as he had in training his hands. Henry never tired of talking golf in the abstract or technical sense although he was by this time reticent, even dismissive, about his own play. Having put all of his life into golf and having achieved his goals, he felt unfulfilled. His golf was in the past tense and he chafed for new conquests.

The disciple became a friend. It was an unlikely friendship

because in many ways we were opposites. He was dazzled by appearances and the trappings of success, a good address, a good car, good clothes, good manners, good connections. Coming from a family of artists, I was broke and bohemian. He sought the company of the rich, the influential and the titled, while I followed my grandfather John Hassall's precept of dividing the world into decent types or dungstarters. I feel sure my grandfather would have judged Henry to be a dungstarter. Henry had his faults but what are faults if not virtues taken to excess? His snobbery amused me and he took an equally forgiving view of my gross deficiencies. Even Toots, with her unbending sense of propriety, tolerated me with the air of a grand duchess excusing a mongrel puppy for peeing on the carpet, scolding but affectionate since I clearly had not received the advantages of proper training. To like people and enjoy their company despite their faults is not a bad definition of friendship and such was the mutual basis of the relationship between myself and the Cottons.

It was, I realised, no kind of qualification for writing a biography. It would be a betrayal of my old friend to write a gushing hagiography. I therefore determined to eliminate myself totally from the task. The book would be based on strictly factual information and the flesh would be added to this skeleton in the form of anecdotes gathered from Henry's friends and acquaintances. It would be pure journalism, with the author rigorously suppressing his own opinions and prejudices and acting purely as a conduit. The evidence would be presented as fully as I could manage and the reader would make his or her own judgments about whether Henry was a decent type or a dungstarter. That plan quickly foundered in the research stages. There were very, very few people around to interview about the early days and the anecdotes I did collect from the later years were so universally sentimental and laced with hero worship that collectively they would have conveyed a false impression. Henry was not a saint and if I was to be true to him I would have to squeeze some corrective drops of lemon juice onto the marzipan.

It proved to be quite the most difficult job of a long writing career. One of the duties of a specialist sports writer is to write obituaries about the game's notable figures and send them in to the newspaper office for use as required. I could never bring myself to write Henry's obit in advance. How could anyone compose himself to such a task when the next post might bring one of his postcards, addressed only to Dobers, Pratts Bottom, England? It is a wonder that the Post Office managed to get those cards to me, an even greater wonder that they bothered, considering the vulgarity of the messages. It was different but no easier after his death because I was drawn even closer to him by being involved in the arrangements for his memorial service and having to visit the stonemason's yard in Portimao to select the marble for his head-stone. The foreman came with me to the graveyard at Mexil-hoeira Grande, a few kilometres along the road from Penina, so that the stone would match Toots' and Nelly's. The place was locked so the foreman had to climb over the railings to take the measurements. By that time one of the outstanding men of British sporting history had been reduced to the stark designation: Plot 337.

There was no point in chiselling an epitaph into that slab of Portuguese marble. A man of this stature could not be encapsu-lated into a few words. It would need a book to do him justice and when the book was finished I was conscious that it was less than a fitting memorial. Henry himself always insisted that he wanted Penina to stand as his memorial and as his definitive statement about the nature of golf. The changes that were made to Penina, without consultation and under his scandalised gaze, not only crushed his spirit but desecrated the course as a memorial. To some extent the course has been restored to Cotton's plan although some of the vandalism remains. For instance, at the time of writing an absurd bunker slap in front of the seventh green mocks the strategic purpose of the original design. Important trees which were removed will take years before their replace-ments perform their full design functions. How I wished that Toots had lived long enough to have routed the despoilers of Henry's magnum opus. Without her flaming spirit to bestir him, Henry suffered the humiliation and heartache without reproach. Intimations of his own mortality made him increasingly diligent in his religious devotions and when we talked about how the changes to the golf course had corrupted the playing quality of the holes his hurt and indignation were punctuated by expressions of for-giveness. It was sad to see the old battler so patently putting his spiritual affairs in order, eliminating all traces of malice from a soul which was soon to be held up to the light for inspection by a higher authority.

Shortly after his death I was called upon to perform one last service for my old friend. Henry had been engaged to design a new course near Penina and he had got no further than drawing a rough routing of which way the holes should run. The client was John Stilwell, the man who had engaged him to build Penina. In view of our long association, I was invited to take over the assignment and help John Stilwell interpret Henry's unspoken ideas. There are many practical considerations which impose their own form on a golf hole. It must be as safe as you can make it from bombardment of people and property outside the course and for the players from stray shots from adjacent holes. It must be accessible for maintenance machinery and suitably contoured for mowing. It must drain freely. The greens, in particular, must not be shrouded from light and air. In Portugal the greens must also be protected from flash-flooding caused by the seasonal torrential rains. At the same time as the designer is solving the problems of these technical imperatives he must juggle with the golfing considerations of balance, strategy, fairness, variety and aesthetics. These golfing elements are very personal to individual architects and as I tramped around the property, banging in posts to mark the sites of tees and greens, discussions with Henry of twenty years previously surfaced like bubbles of marsh gas bursting through the sludge of my turgid memory.

Golf can never be completely fair but it should be as fair as the architect can make it.

The punishment for stray shots should be graduated to fit the crime. But they must be punished, otherwise it is unfair to an opponent who plays a good shot. So the rewards for good shots must also be graduated to fit the degree of virtuosity.

Golf should be a pleasure and there is no fun in searching for balls in penal rough. A hole that depends on heavy rough for its defences is a badly designed hole.

Golf should be like chess in that the player should be required to identify the right move from several options before he plays the shot.

The golfer has no divine right to the use of the driver off the tee. Many second-rate professionals have criticised the fifth at Penina because they can't use the driver on a par-five. Actually it is an easy par-five for any golfer who has the nous to work out how to play it.

One of the main pleasures of golf is simply being in beautiful surroundings, remote from the real world. At Penina I tried to create the impression that the golfer and his companions were alone in a forest glade.

Dead straight holes are boring. Even a slight change of direction creates a vista which draws the golfer forward.

Every hole should be playable and enjoyable for every category of golfer from the learner to the expert.

A low score is not a reproof to the designer; it is a compliment to the greenkeeper.

Many of these principles are universal truths of golf, although often flouted in modern design for the sake of sensationalism, and individual architects put their personal stamp on a course by the way they interpret and execute the basic precepts. It would be excessively fanciful to suggest that I acted like a medium, still less like a Joan of Arc, in hearing voices as I worked on the Alto Club at Alvor. But I was aware of his strictures as I shaped the greens and sited the bunkers and in certain areas I did things Henry's way when I would have done something quite different if left to my own devices. Seeing that course take shape was just about the most satisfying experience of my life, even though I did have to destroy a vineyard in the process. Others must judge whether the course it Cottonesque. I do not suppose that Henry would have approved every detail of his last course, any more than Schubert would have approved the completion of his Unfinished Symphony. But at least it will stand as a permanent source of pleasure for many thousands of golfers and as a tangible legacy of a man who made a massive contribution to the game of golf.

As to that contribution, it took many forms. He was not, as he is sometimes portrayed, an idealist fired by zeal to reform the world of golf. He simply wanted a better world for Henry Cotton, but he understood full well that others would follow along the trail he pioneered. He employed hard work to raise the standards of his own golf and others perforce had to raise theirs. He employed mockery to destroy the snobbish barriers which were erected to keep him in a state of servility and his brother professionals were emancipated in the process. He started what was to become the massive industry of player sponsorship and endorsements. Above all, he set standards of behaviour and rewards to inspire the ambitions of succeeding generations.

It is widely believed in golf, especially among selection committees, that golfers possess a finite reservoir of nervous fortitude and enthusiasm for battle. Players are dropped from teams not on the grounds of diminishing skill but because it is suspected that they have exhausted their ration of holing vital putts and mounting counter-attacks. In Henry's case the game went first as age and ill health took their toll. And then, as it appeared to me, a weariness came over him. He slackened his grip. As a young man his preparations for golf were more meticulous and physically demanding than any other golfer had ever contemplated. Under the insistence of Toots he brought the same thoroughness and application to everything he did, from furnishing a house, to making radio broadcasts, to buying a motor car. But that habit of whole-heartedness vanished when his playing days ended and he became really rather slipshod in his commercial activities and interested only in the rewards. But in one area of his life he remained as diligent and committed as ever right to the end. He had a passionate ambition to pass on the knowledge and skills he had acquired so painfully and nothing fired his enthusiasm so much as the visit to Penina of a young player in search of enlightenment. By the time he was in his seventies he was no more than a name in the history books to a twenty-year-old and it is a natural conceit of youth to believe that nobody from a previous generation could play worth a lick compared to the modern superstars.

Henry understood this attitude and so he habitually started his lessons by establishing his credibility as a player and teacher. His party trick of hitting a succession of one-handed shots without regripping the club, an exercise very few if any of today's superstars could reproduce, has been described earlier. He had another routine which was equally impressive to advanced students of golf. He would take a club, usually his four-wood, and explain that he was going to hit a number of shots. The pupils were to watch him make the stroke and as soon as the ball was struck they were to call out their judgment of whether it was a short, medium or long shot. Before the balls landed Cotton would announce the distances: 175 yards, 220 yards, 200 yards, 250 yards. Nobody ever made much of a fist of this test because it was impossible to discern any change in Henry's action. He would then explain: "The quickness of the hand deceives the eye," and the pupils would be in a totally receptive frame of mind to absorb his familiar homily on the paramount importance of well-trained hands. As always in discussions about Henry Cotton, the focus of interest has come round to those hands. They symbolised the strength and significance of his life as a golfer, marking the gulf which separates the elite band of immortals who play golf as opposed to the millions who play at golf. That is the most important point I have sought to establish in this book. As for the multi-faceted personality of the man, my original plan of leaving the reader to make an individual judgment must stand. But from my biased perspective he was more of a decent type, much more, than a dungstarter.

APPENDICES

The Golfer

Career Victories

1925 Kent Professional championship
1927 Kent Professional championship
1928 Kent Professional championship, Croydon and District
     Professional championship
1930 Kent Professional championship, Mar del Plata Open
     (Argentina), Belgian Open
1931 Dunlop Southport tournament
1932 Dunlop Southport tournament, PGA championship
1934 Belgian Open, OPEN CHAMPIONSHIP
1935 Leeds tournament, Yorkshire Evening News tournament
1936 Italian Open, Dunlop Metropolitan tournament
1937 German Open, Silver King tournament, Czechoslovakian
     Open, OPEN CHAMPIONSHIP
1938 Belgian Open, German Open, Czechoslovakian Open
1939 German Open, Daily Mail tournament, Penfold League
     tournament
1940 PGA championship
1945 News Chronicle tournament
1946 PGA championship, French Open, Star tournament,
     Vichy Open
1947 French Open, Spalding tournament, Yorkshire Evening
     News tournament
1948 OPEN CHAMPIONSHIP, White Sulphur Springs
     Invitational (USA)
1953 Dunlop 2,000 Guineas tournament
1954 Penfold 1,000 Guineas tournament
1956 Metropolitan Qualifying tournament, US Open

The Author

Books by Henry Cotton

Golf, Eyre and Spottiswoode 1931.
This Game of Golf, Country Life 1948.
My Swing, Country Life 1952.
My Golfing Album, Country Life 1959.
Henry Cotton Says, Country Life 1962.
Study the Game of Golf with Henry Cotton, Country Life 1964.
Henry Cotton's Guide to Golf in the British Isles, Cliveden
    Press 1969.
Play Better Golf, David and Charles 1973 (Revised edition of
    Henry Cotton Says).
Golf: A Pictorial History, Collins 1975.
Thanks for the Game, Sidgwick and Jackson 1980.

The Golf Course Architect

Courses designed by Henry Cotton

Great Britain: Abridge, Ampfield, Beamish Park, Canons
  Brook, Ely City, Farnham Park, Folly Hill, Sene Valley,
  Windmill Hill, Gourock, Moray, Windyhill, St Mellons.
France: Mont d'Arbois.
Italy: Bergamo L'Albenza, Bologna, Tirrenia, Torino.
Madeira Islands: Santo da Serra.
Portugal: Monte Gordo, Penina, Vale do Lobo, Alto Club.

Courses revised by Henry Cotton

La Moye, Castle Eden, Eaglescliffe, Felixstowe Ferry, Royal
Cinque Ports, Temple, Langley Park, Deauville, Campo Carlo
Magno, Lido de Venezia, Stirling, Puerto de Hierro.